DASH 1

FOR BEGINNERS

Cookbook

The Simplest and Quickest **120+ Dietary Approach Recipes** to Stop Hypertension! Increase your Heart Health and **Reduce Cholesterol** and Triglycerides with One of **the Healthiest Diets Overall**!

By

Michelle Sandler

Table of Contents

Introduction to Dietary Approaches to Stop Hypertension

The DASH Diet is a simple and easy dietary regimen specifically for **heart health**. It is one of the few diets in the world specifically designed to reduce triglycerides and bad cholesterol in the blood, in order to improve blood pressure and blood circulation. Indeed, the aim of the DASH diet is to improve the health of all the persons who follow it. After careful clinical studies conducted in the United States, the Dash Diet is currently recommended by many medical associations in the world, especially for all of people at risk of developing cardiovascular disease.

DASH is an acronym: it stands for *Dietary Approaches to Stop Hypertension.*

Dash Diet is not linked to weight loss. In fact, the number of calories introduced is equal to the daily nutritional requirements (it is a so-called isocaloric diet) and not less.

However, there are some **variants of the Dash Diet** specific for overweight people, based on the consumption of the same foods but in smaller portions in order to reduce the calories acquired.

What are the additional benefits of following the DASH diet?

Clinical studies show that a high consumption of fruits and vegetables reduces the risk of developing **diabetes**, **cancer, atherosclerosis**, and other diseases typical of old age.

Replacing saturated fats, found in butter or cheese, with unsaturated fats, found in nuts, olive oil, and seeds, helps reduce triglycerides and cholesterol, greatly reducing the chance of developing cardiovascular disease.

Anyone can follow the Dash Diet: *women*, *kids*, *athletes*, *older people*, *sedentary people* and *men*!

I think all of us should follow this diet to have a much healthier lifestyle and live better and longer. Due the simplicity of this diet, I wanted to create this fantastic cookbook: *I wanted to collect the simplest and quickest 120 Dash Recipes for all people who wat to start this dietary regimen, even if they have never known and even if they start by basics!*

Dash Diet involves eating certain foods and reducing (or sometimes eliminating) others.

Yes foods:
- Vegetables
- Carbohydrates from whole grains
- Fruit
- Low-fat dairy products
- Fish
- White meat
- Vegetable oils
- Sea Salt/Himalayan salt

No foods:
- Red meat
- Animal fats
- Sugar
- Alcohol
- Processed products
- Synthetic salt (sodium chloride)
- Preservatives

Chapter 1· BREAKFAST

AND SNACKS

1) ROASTED RED PEPPERS AND PESTO OMELETTE

Preparation Time: 10 minutes	**Cooking Time**: 20 minutes	**Servings: 4**

Ingredients:

- ✓ 8 big eggs
- ✓ ¼ cup store-bought pesto
- ✓ ¼ teaspoon ground black pepper
- ✓ ⅛ teaspoon of kosher salt or sea salt

Ingredients:

- ✓ Kitchen spray
- ✓ ½ cup of spinach leaves
- ✓ ½ cup jarred roasted red peppers, chopped
- ✓ ¾ cup shredded white Cheddar cheese

Directions:

- ❖ Heat a large nonstick skillet over medium-low heat.
- ❖ In a medium bowl, whisk together the eggs, pesto, black pepper and salt until well combined.
- ❖ Coat the skillet with cooking spray. Add ¼ of the spinach and stir until slightly wilted. Pour in ¼ of the egg mixture. Let cook for 2 to 3 minutes, until the egg is almost set. Place ¼ of the roasted red peppers and cheese in the center of the omelet.

- ❖ Fold the omelet in half. Put a lid on and cook for 1 to 2 minutes, until the cheese is melted.
- ❖ Repeat step 3 with remaining ingredients to make 4 omelets total.
- ❖ Store omelets in airtight microwave-safe containers and refrigerate for up to 5 days. Microwave on high speed for 2 minutes, until heated through.

2) MUSHROOM OMELETTE

Preparation Time: 15 minutes	**Cooking Time**: 25 minutes	**Servings: 6**

Ingredients:

- ✓ 12 big eggs
- ✓ ½ cup low-fat Greek yogurt
- ✓ 1 tablespoon of balsamic vinegar
- ✓ ¾ teaspoon of kosher salt or sea salt
- ✓ ¼ teaspoon ground black pepper
- ✓ 1½ cups shredded Swiss cheese, split

Ingredients:

- ✓ 3 tablespoons of olive oil
- ✓ 1 large shallot, peeled and thinly sliced
- ✓ 2 shallots, thinly sliced
- ✓ 2 cups of sliced mushrooms
- ✓ 2 teaspoons of chopped fresh thyme leaves

Directions:

- ❖ Preheat the oven to 375ºF (190ºC).
- ❖ In a large bowl, whisk together the eggs, Greek yogurt, balsamic vinegar, salt, black pepper and half of the shredded Swiss cheese until well combined.
- ❖ Heat the olive oil in a large nonstick ovenproof skillet over medium heat. Add the shallots, scallions and mushrooms and sauté 4 to 5 minutes, until the mushrooms are soft. Add the thyme.

- ❖ Pour egg mixture into skillet with mushroom mixture and cook 4 to 5 minutes, until bottom begins to set. Top with the remaining shredded cheese and transfer to the oven. Bake for 15 minutes, until the egg has set.
- ❖ Remove the omelet from the oven and let it cool slightly, then cut it into 6 wedges.
- ❖ Store omelet slices in airtight microwave-safe containers and refrigerate for up to 5 days. Microwave on high speed for 60-90 seconds, until heated through.

	3) MAPLE SWEET POTATO PANCAKES	
Preparation Time: 15 minutes	**Cooking Time:** 20 minutes	**Servings: 6**

Ingredients:

- ✓ 2 cups whole wheat flour or whole wheat pasta flour
- ✓ 1 tablespoon baking powder
- ✓ 1½ teaspoons pumpkin pie spice
- ✓ ½ teaspoon of kosher salt or sea salt
- ✓ 2 tablespoons of dark brown sugar
- ✓ 4 tablespoons of canola oil
- ✓ 2 big eggs

Ingredients:

- ✓ 1 cup mashed sweet potatoes or cooked mashed sweet potatoes
- ✓ 1½ cups of skimmed milk
- ✓ 1 teaspoon of pure vanilla extract
- ✓ Kitchen spray
- ✓ 1½ cups of fat-free Greek yogurt
- ✓ ½ teaspoon of maple extract or 1 tablespoon of pure maple syrup

Directions:

- ❖ In a bowl, whisk together the flour, baking powder, pumpkin pie spice and salt until combined.
- ❖ In a separate bowl, use a hand mixer set on medium speed to beat the brown sugar and canola oil together until fluffy. While the hand mixer is still beating, add one egg at a time until fully combined. Add the sweet potato puree, then the milk and vanilla extract until well combined. Turn the hand mixer to low speed and slowly add the dry ingredient mixture until well combined.

- ❖ Heat a large nonstick skillet over medium heat. Coat the skillet with cooking spray. Working in batches, pour ¼ cup piles of pancake batter into the pan. Cook for 1 to 2 minutes, until bubbles appear on top, then flip and cook for another 1 to 2 minutes, until set. Repeat with remaining batter.
- ❖ In a small bowl, whisk together the Greek yogurt and maple extract or maple syrup until combined. Serve on top of the sweet potato pancakes.
- ❖ Store pancakes in the refrigerator in an airtight container or sealed plastic bag for up to 5 days. Serve chilled or reheat in the microwave on high speed for 30 seconds. Store maple yogurt in an airtight container for up to 5 days.

	4) FLAX WAFFLES WITH STRAWBERRY PUREE	
Preparation Time: 15 minutes	**Cooking Time:** 15 minutes	**Servings: 6**

Ingredients:

- ✓ 1 quart of strawberries, hulled and chopped
- ✓ 1 cup of water
- ✓ 2 spoons of honey
- ✓ 2½ teaspoons of pure vanilla extract, split
- ✓ 2¼ cups whole wheat flour or whole wheat pasta flour
- ✓ ¼ cup ground flaxseed
- ✓ 2½ teaspoons baking powder

Ingredients:

- ✓ 1 teaspoon of baking soda
- ✓ ½ teaspoon of kosher salt or sea salt
- ✓ 2 teaspoons ground cinnamon
- ✓ 2 tablespoons of dark brown sugar
- ✓ ¼ cup canola oil
- ✓ 3 big eggs
- ✓ 1 cup of skimmed milk
- ✓ Kitchen spray

- ❖ First, make the strawberry puree: Place the strawberries, water, honey, and ½ teaspoon vanilla extract in a medium saucepan and bring to a boil for 5-6 minutes, until the strawberries are soft. Use an immersion blender to puree the strawberries or transfer the mixture to a blender and puree until smooth.
- ❖ To make the waffles: In a medium bowl, whisk together the flour, flaxseed, baking powder, baking soda, and salt until combined.
- ❖ In a large bowl, whisk together ground cinnamon, brown sugar and canola oil until well combined. Beat in one egg at a time until the mixture is frothy. Add the remaining vanilla extract and milk until combined. Slowly

- ❖ Heat a Belgian waffle maker over medium heat. Once hot, coat with cooking spray. Pour 2/3 cup of batter evenly into the waffle maker. Close the lid and cook for 1½ to 2 minutes, until the waffle is golden brown on the outside. Repeat with the remaining batter.
- ❖ Serve the waffles with the strawberry puree.
- ❖ Store waffles in the refrigerator in an airtight container or sealed plastic bag for up to 5 days. Serve chilled or reheat in the microwave on high speed for 30 seconds. Store strawberry puree in an airtight container for up to 5 days.

whisk the dry ingredients into the wet mixture.

5) BAKED EGGS WITH CHARD AND FETA CHEESE

Preparation Time: 15 minutes	**Cooking Time**: 10 to 15 minutes	**Servings**: 4

Ingredients:

- ✓ 1 tablespoon of extra virgin olive oil, divided
- ✓ ½ red onion, diced
- ✓ ½ teaspoon of kosher salt
- ✓ ¼ teaspoon of nutmeg
- ✓ ⅛ teaspoon of freshly ground black pepper

Ingredients:

- ✓ 4 cups chopped beets
- ✓ ¼ cup of crumbled feta cheese
- ✓ 4 big eggs
- ✓ ¼ cup fresh basil, chopped or cut into ribbons

Directions:

❖ Preheat oven to 375°F (190°C). Place 4 ramekins on a half or full baking sheet and lightly grease them with olive oil.

❖ Heat the remaining olive oil in a large skillet or frying pan over medium heat. Add the onion, salt, nutmeg, and pepper and sauté until translucent, about 3 minutes. Add the chard and cook, stirring, until wilted, about 2 minutes.

❖ Divide the mixture among the 4 ramekins. Add 1 tablespoon feta cheese to each ramekin. Crack 1 egg on top of the mixture in each ramekin. Bake for 10-12 minutes, or until egg whites have set.

❖ Let cool for 1 to 2 minutes, then carefully transfer eggs from ramekins to a plate with a fork or spatula. Garnish with the basil.

6) SHAKSHUKA WITH HARISSA AND TOMATOES

Preparation Time: 10 minutes	**Cooking Time**: 20 minutes	**Servings**: 4

Ingredients:

- ✓ 1½ tablespoons of extra virgin olive oil
- ✓ 2 tablespoons of harissa
- ✓ 1 tablespoon of tomato paste
- ✓ ½ onion, diced
- ✓ 1 bell pepper, seeded and diced

Ingredients:

- ✓ 3 garlic cloves, minced
- ✓ 1 (28-ounce / 794-g) can no salt added diced tomatoes
- ✓ ½ teaspoon of kosher salt
- ✓ 4 big eggs
- ✓ 2 or 3 tablespoons of fresh basil, chopped or cut into ribbons

Directions:

❖ Preheat the oven to 375°F (190°C).

❖ Heat olive oil in a 12-inch cast iron skillet or ovenproof pan over medium heat. Add the harissa, tomato paste, onion and bell bell pepper; sauté for 3 to 4 minutes. Add the garlic and cook until fragrant, about 30 seconds.

❖ Add the diced tomatoes and salt and simmer for about 10 minutes.

❖ Make 4 wells in the sauce and gently crack 1 egg into each. Transfer to the oven and bake until the whites are cooked through and the yolks are set, 10 to 12 minutes.

❖ Allow to cool 3 to 5 minutes, garnish with basil and carefully distribute to plates.

7) SCRAMBLED EGGS WITH SMOKED SALMON		
Preparation Time: 5 minutes	**Cooking Time:** 5 minutes	**Servings: 2**

Ingredients:

- ✓ 4 big eggs
- ✓ 1 tablespoon of milk
- ✓ 1 tablespoon chopped fresh chives
- ✓ 1 tablespoon chopped fresh dill

Ingredients:

- ✓ ¼ teaspoon of kosher salt
- ✓ ⅛ teaspoon of freshly ground black pepper
- ✓ 2 teaspoons of extra virgin olive oil
- ✓ 2 ounces (57 g) of smoked salmon, thinly sliced

Directions:

- ❖ In a large bowl, whisk together the eggs, milk, chives, dill, salt and pepper.
- ❖ Heat the olive oil in a medium skillet over medium heat.

- ❖ Add the egg mixture and cook for about 3 minutes, stirring occasionally.
- ❖ Add the salmon and cook until the eggs are set but moist, about 1 minute.

8) FIGS TOAST WITH HONEY AND RICOTTA CHEESE		
Preparation Time: 5 minutes	**Cooking Time:** 0 minutes	**Servings: 2**

Ingredients:

- ✓ ¼ cup of cottage cheese
- ✓ 2 pieces of wholemeal bread, toasted
- ✓ 4 figs, halved

Ingredients:

- ✓ 2 tablespoons chopped walnuts
- ✓ 1 teaspoon of honey

Directions:

- ❖ Spread 2 tablespoons ricotta cheese on each piece of toast. Add 4 fig halves to each piece of toast, pressing firmly to keep figs in ricotta.

- ❖ Sprinkle 1 tablespoon walnuts and pour ½ teaspoon honey over each piece of toast.

Chapter 2. LUNCH

9) BALELA SALAD FROM THE MIDDLE EAST

Preparation Time:	Cooking Time: 0 minutes	Servings: 6

Ingredients:

- ✓ 1 jalapeno, finely chopped (optional)
- ✓ 1/2 green bell pepper, cored and chopped
- ✓ 2 1/2 cups grape tomatoes, halved
- ✓ 1/2 cup sun-dried tomatoes
- ✓ 1/2 cup chopped fresh parsley
- ✓ 1/2 cup chopped fresh mint or basil leaves
- ✓ 1/3 cup pitted Kalamata olives
- ✓ 1/4 cup pitted green olives
- ✓ 3 1/2 cups cooked chickpeas, drained and rinsed
- ✓ 3-5 green onions, both white and green, chopped

Ingredients:

Ingredients for the dressing:

- ✓ 1 garlic clove, minced
- ✓ 1 teaspoon ground sumac
- ✓ 1/2 teaspoon Aleppo pepper
- ✓ 1/4 cup Early Harvest Greek extra virgin olive oil
- ✓ 1/4 to 1/2 teaspoon crushed red pepper (optional)
- ✓ 2 tablespoons lemon juice
- ✓ 2 tablespoons white wine vinegar
- ✓ Salt and black pepper, a generous pinch to your taste

Directions:

- ❖ Mix salad ingredients in a large salad bowl.
- ❖ In a separate smaller bowl or jar, mix together the dressing ingredients.

- ❖ Pour dressing over salad and toss gently to coat.
- ❖ Set aside for 30 minutes to allow flavors to blend. Serve and enjoy.

10) GRILLED TOMATO AND BROCCOLI SALAD

Preparation Time: 20 minutes	Cooking Time:	Servings: 6

Ingredients:

- ✓ ¼ cup lemon juice
- ✓ ½ teaspoon chili powder
- ✓ 1 pound and a half boneless chicken breast
- ✓ 1 pound and a half medium tomato

Ingredients:

- ✓ 1 teaspoon freshly ground pepper
- ✓ 1 teaspoon salt
- ✓ 4 cups broccoli florets
- ✓ 5 tablespoons extra virgin olive oil, divided into 2 and 3 tablespoons

Directions:

- ❖ Place the chicken in a skillet and add enough water to cover the chicken. Bring to a boil over high heat.
- ❖ Reduce the heat once the liquid boils and cook the chicken thoroughly for 12 minutes.
- ❖ Once cooked, shred the chicken into bite-sized pieces. In a large pot, bring the water to a boil and add the broccoli. Cook for 5 minutes until slightly tender.
- ❖ Drain and rinse broccoli with cold water. Set aside. Twist the tomatoes and cut them crosswise.

- ❖ Discard seeds and place cut tomatoes on paper towels. Pat them dry. In a heavy skillet, heat the skillet over high heat until very hot.
- ❖ Brush the cut sides of the tomatoes with olive oil and place them on the skillet.
- ❖ Cook the tomatoes until the sides are charred. Set aside. In the same skillet, heat the remaining 3 tablespoons of olive oil over medium heat.
- ❖ Stir in the salt, chili powder and pepper and stir for 45 seconds. Pour in the lemon juice and remove the skillet from the heat.
- ❖ Plate the broccoli, shredded chicken and seasoning from the chili powder mixture

11) ASIAN STYLE COLESLAW

Preparation Time: 0 minutes	**Cooking Time:**	**Servings: 10**

Ingredients:

- ✓ ½ cup chopped fresh cilantro
- ✓ 1 ½ tablespoons chopped garlic
- ✓ 2 carrots, julienned
- ✓ 2 cups shredded napa cabbage
- ✓ 2 cups thinly sliced red cabbage
- ✓ 2 red peppers
- ✓ 2 tablespoons chopped fresh ginger root

Ingredients:

- ✓ 3 tablespoons brown sugar
- ✓ 3 tablespoons soy sauce
- ✓ 5 cups thinly sliced green cabbage
- ✓ 5 tablespoons creamy peanut butter
- ✓ 6 chopped green onions
- ✓ 6 tablespoons rice wine vinegar
- ✓ 6 tablespoons vegetable oil

❖ Pour in the above peanut sauce and mix well. Serve and enjoy.

Directions:

❖ Thoroughly mix the following in a medium bowl: garlic, ginger, brown sugar, soy sauce, peanut butter, oil and rice vinegar.

❖ In a separate bowl, thoroughly mix cilantro, green onions, carrots, bell bell pepper, Napa cabbage, red cabbage and green cabbage.

12) EASY QUINOA AND PEAR SALAD

Preparation Time: 0 minutes	**Cooking Time:**	**Servings: 6**

Ingredients:

- ✓ ¼ cup chopped parsley
- ✓ ¼ cup chopped shallots
- ✓ ¼ cup lime juice
- ✓ ¼ cup red onion, diced
- ✓ ½ cup diced carrots
- ✓ ½ cup diced celery
- ✓ ½ cup diced cucumber
- ✓ ½ cup diced red bell bell pepper

Ingredients:

- ✓ ½ cup dried wild blueberries
- ✓ ½ cup olive oil
- ✓ ½ cup spicy pecans, chopped
- ✓ 1 tablespoon chopped parsley
- ✓ 1 teaspoon honey
- ✓ 1 teaspoon sea salt
- ✓ 2 fresh pears, chopped
- ✓ 3 cups cooked quinoa

❖ Set aside. In a large salad bowl, add remaining ingredients and mix well.

❖ Pour over dressing and toss well to coat. Serve and enjoy.

Directions:

❖ In a small bowl mix well olive oil, salt, lime juice, honey and parsley.

13) VEGETARIAN EGG CUPCAKES		
Preparation Time: 30 minutes	**Cooking Time**:	**Servings**: 2

Ingredients:

- ✓ ¼ cup cabbage, shredded
- ✓ 3 eggs
- ✓ 1 leek, sliced
- ✓ 4 tablespoons parmesan cheese, grated

Ingredients:

- ✓ 2 tablespoons almond milk
- ✓ 1 red bell pepper, shredded Salt and black pepper to taste
- ✓ 1 tomato, shredded
- ✓ 2 tablespoons mozzarella cheese, grated

Directions:

- ❖ Preheat oven to 360 F. Grease a muffin pan with cooking spray. Beat the eggs in a bowl.
- ❖ Add the milk, cabbage, leek, Parmesan cheese, bell bell pepper, salt, black pepper, tomato and cheddar cheese and mix.

- ❖ Divide the mixture between the molds and bake for 20-25 minutes. Allow to cool completely on a wire rack before serving.

14) FENNEL AND PEAR SALAD WITH ENDIVE		
Preparation Time: 5 minutes	**Cooking Time**:	**Servings**: 4

Ingredients:

- ✓ 2 tablespoons olive oil
- ✓ 1 tablespoon balsamic vinegar
- ✓ 2 cloves garlic, minced
- ✓ 1 tablespoon Dijon mustard
- ✓ 1 tablespoon lemon juice Sea salt and black pepper to taste

Ingredients:

- ✓ ½ cup black olives, pitted and chopped
- ✓ 1 tablespoon parsley, chopped
- ✓ 7 cups spinach
- ✓ 2 endives, chopped
- ✓ 2 pears, sliced lengthwise
- ✓ 2 fennel bulbs, chopped

Directions:

- ❖ Put spinach, endive, pears, fennel, parsley, olives, salt, pepper, lemon juice, olive oil, mustard, garlic and balsamic vinegar in a bowl and mix. Serve immediately.

15) SPINACH AND BULGUR PIES

Preparation Time: 45 minutes	Cooking Time:	Servings: 6

Ingredients:

- ✓ 2 eggs, beaten
- ✓ 1 cup bulgur
- ✓ 3 cups water
- ✓ 1 cup spinach, torn
- ✓ 2 spring onions, chopped

Ingredients:

- ✓ ¼ cup pecorino cheese, grated
- ✓ ½ teaspoon garlic powder Sea salt and black pepper to taste
- ✓ ½ teaspoon dried oregano

Directions:

- ❖ Preheat oven to 340 F.
- ❖ Grease a muffin pan with cooking spray. Heat 2 cups of salted water in a saucepan over medium heat and add the bulgur.

- ❖ Bring to a boil and cook for 10-15 minutes. Remove to a bowl and stir with a fork.
- ❖ Add the spinach, spring onions, eggs, pecorino cheese, garlic powder, salt, pepper and oregano.
- ❖ Divide between the muffin holes and bake for 25 minutes. Serve fresh.

16) BASIL TOMATO EGG SKILLET

Preparation Time: 25 minutes	Cooking Time:	Servings: 2

Ingredients:

- ✓ 2 tablespoons olive oil
- ✓ 2 beaten eggs
- ✓ 2 diced tomatoes

Ingredients:

- ✓ 1 tablespoon chopped basil
- ✓ 1 chopped green onion Salt and black pepper to taste

Directions:

- ❖ Heat olive oil in a skillet over medium heat and sauté tomatoes, green onion, salt and pepper for 5 minutes.

- ❖ Add eggs and cook for another 10 minutes. Serve topped with basil.

17) LETTUCE SALAD WITH APPLES AND WALNUTS

Preparation Time: 5 minutes	Cooking Time:	Servings: 4

Ingredients:

- ✓ 1 apple, peeled and chopped
- ✓ 1 head of Iceberg lettuce, torn
- ✓ 1 tablespoon apple cider vinegar
- ✓ 2 tablespoons olive oil

Ingredients:

- ✓ 2 tablespoons walnuts, chopped
- ✓ 1 tomato, sliced
- ✓ 8 olives stuffed with anchovies Salt to taste

Directions:

- ❖ Combine the lettuce, apple cider vinegar, olive oil, apple and walnuts in a salad bowl.

- ❖ Stir to coat. Add the tomato and olives and serve immediately.

18) BREAD WITH POPPY SEEDS, OLIVES AND CHEESE

Preparation Time: 40 minutes + leavening time	Cooking Time:	Servings: 6

Ingredients:

- ¼ cup olive oil
- 4 cups whole-wheat flour
- 3 tablespoons oregano, chopped
- 2 tablespoons dry yeast
- 1 cup black olives, pitted and sliced

Ingredients:

- 1 cup warm water
- ½ cup feta cheese, crumbled
- 1 tablespoon poppy seeds
- 1 egg, beaten

- In a bowl, combine the flour, water, yeast and olive oil and knead the dough well.
- Transfer to a bowl and let rest covered with plastic wrap to rise until doubled in size for 60 minutes.
- Remove plastic wrap and add oregano, black olives and feta cheese. Place on a floured surface and knead again. Form dough into 6 balls and place in lined baking dish.

- Cover and let rise for an additional 40 minutes.
- Preheat oven to 390 F. Brush the balls with the egg and sprinkle with the poppy seeds.
- Bake for 25-30 minutes. Serve.

19) RICOTTA OMELETTE WITH BERRIES

Preparation Time: 10 minutes	Cooking Time:	Servings: 4

Ingredients:

- 2 tablespoons olive oil
- 6 beaten eggs
- 1 teaspoon cinnamon powder

Ingredients:

- 1 cup cottage cheese
- 4 ounces berries

- Whisk the eggs, cinnamon powder, cottage cheese and berries in a bowl.
- Heat the olive oil in a skillet over medium heat and pour in the egg mixture.

- Cook for 2 minutes, flip the egg and cook for another 2 minutes. Serve immediately.

20) ROASTED CAULIFLOWER WITH MUSHROOMS

Preparation Time: 35 minutes	Cooking Time:	Servings: 4

- 2 tablespoons olive oil
- 4 cups cauliflower florets
- 1 celery stalk, chopped
- 1 cup white mushrooms, sliced

- 1 cup cherry tomatoes, halved
- 1 yellow onion, chopped
- 2 cloves garlic, chopped
- 2 tablespoons dill, chopped Salt and black pepper to taste

- Preheat oven to 340 F. Line a baking sheet with parchment paper.
- Toss in cauliflower florets, olive oil, mushrooms, celery, tomatoes, onion, garlic, salt and pepper and stir to combine.

- Bake for 25 minutes. Serve topped with dill.

21) BACON AND EGG CRUMBLE		
Preparation Time: 1 hour and 15 minutes	**Cooking Time:**	**Servings:** 4
✓ 4 eggs, beaten ✓ 1 red onion, chopped ✓ 3 ounces bacon, chopped ✓ 2 cloves garlic, chopped	✓ 2 tablespoons olive oil ✓ 2 ounces goat cheese, crumbled ✓ 1 tablespoon basil, chopped Salt and black pepper to taste	
❖ Heat half the oil in a skillet over medium heat and sauté the onion, bacon and garlic for 3 minutes. ❖ Add the goat cheese and beaten eggs and cook for 5-6 minutes, stirring often. Season with salt and pepper.	❖ Sprinkle with basil and serve.	

22) ITALIAN RICE AND SPINACH SALAD		
Preparation Time: 30 minutes	**Cooking Time:**	**Servings:** 2
✓ 1 tablespoon olive oil ✓ Salt and black pepper to taste ✓ ½ cup baby spinach ✓ ½ cup green peas, blanched ✓ 1 clove garlic, minced	✓ ½ cup white rice, rinsed ✓ ½ cup cherry tomatoes, halved ✓ 1 tablespoon parsley, chopped ✓ 2 tablespoons Italian salad dressing	
❖ Bring a large pot of salted water to a boil over medium heat. Pour in rice, cover and cook over low heat for 15-18 minutes or until rice is al dente. ❖ Drain and let cool in a salad bowl. In a bowl, whisk the olive oil, garlic, salt and black pepper.	❖ Combine the green peas, spinach and rice. Pour the dressing over everything and toss gently to combine. ❖ Decorate with cherry tomatoes and parsley and serve. Enjoy!	

23) FRUITY ASPARAGUS AND QUINOA SALAD		
Preparation Time: 25 minutes	**Cooking Time:**	**Servings:** 8
✓ ¼ cup chopped pecans, toasted ✓ ½ cup finely chopped white onion ✓ ½ jalapeno bell pepper, diced ✓ ½ pound asparagus, steamed and cooled ✓ ½ teaspoon kosher salt ✓ 1 cup fresh orange sections ✓ 1 cup uncooked quinoa ✓ 1 tablespoon olive oil ✓ 2 cups water	✓ 2 tablespoons chopped red onion ✓ 5 dates, pitted and chopped SEASONING INGREDIENTS: ✓ ¼ teaspoon ground black pepper ✓ ¼ teaspoon kosher salt 1 clove minced garlic ✓ 1 tablespoon olive oil ✓ 2 tablespoons chopped fresh mint ✓ 2 tablespoons fresh lemon juice Sprigs of mint - optional	
❖ Wash and hand scrub quinoa in a bowl at least three times, discarding water each time. ❖ Over medium-high heat, place a large nonstick skillet and heat 1 tablespoon olive oil. ❖ For two minutes, sauté the onions before adding the quinoa and sautéing for another five minutes. ❖ Add ½ teaspoon salt and 2 cups water and bring to a boil. Lower the heat to a simmer, cover and cook for 15 minutes.	❖ Turn off the heat and let stand until the water is absorbed. Add the pepper, asparagus, dates, pecans and orange sections to a salad bowl. ❖ Add the cooked quinoa; mix well. In a small bowl, whisk the mint, garlic, black pepper, salt, olive oil and lemon juice to create the dressing. ❖ Pour the dressing over the salad, serve and enjoy.	

24) CITRUS SALAD DRESSED WITH GINGER YOGURT

Preparation Time: 1 hour	Cooking Time:	Servings: 6

Ingredients:	Ingredients:
✓ 2/3 cup ground crystallized ginger ✓ 1 16-ounce Greek yogurt ✓ ¼ teaspoon cinnamon powder ✓ 2 tablespoons honey	✓ ½ cup dried cranberries ✓ 3 navel oranges ✓ 2 large tangerines, peeled ✓ 1 pink grapefruit, peeled
❖ In sections, break up the mandarins and grapefruit. Cut mandarin sections in half. In thirds, slice grapefruit sections. ❖ Cut orange pith and peel in half and slice oranges into ¼-inch-thick rounds, then into quarters. In a medium bowl, mix the oranges, grapefruit, tangerines and their juices.	❖ Add the cinnamon, honey, and ½ cup of the blueberries. Cover and refrigerate for 1 hour. ❖ In a small bowl, mix the ginger and yogurt. ❖ To serve, add a spoonful of yogurt dressing to a serving of fruit and sprinkle with blueberries.

25) GRILLED HALLOUMI CHEESE SALAD

Preparation Time: 10 minutes	Cooking Time:	Servings: 1

✓ 0.5 ounces chopped walnuts ✓ 1 handful arugula ✓ 1 Persian cucumber, cut into circles about	✓ ½ inch thick ✓ 3 ounces halloumi cheese ✓ 5 grape tomatoes, cut in half balsamic vinegar olive oil salt
❖ In 1/3 slices, cut cheese. ❖ For 3 to 5 minutes each side, grill types of cheese until grill marks show. In a salad bowl, add arugula, cucumber and tomatoes.	❖ Drizzle with olive oil and balsamic vinegar. ❖ Season with salt and toss well. Sprinkle with walnuts and add the grilled halloumi. Serve and enjoy.

26) GLUTEN-FREE FOCACCIA WITH GARLIC AND TOMATO

Preparation Time: 20 minutes	Cooking Time:	Servings: 8

✓ 1 egg ✓ ½ tablespoon lemon juice ✓ 1 tablespoon honey ✓ 4 tablespoons olive oil A pinch of sugar ✓ 1 ¼ cup warm water ✓ 1 tablespoon active dry yeast ✓ 2 tablespoons rosemary, chopped ✓ 2 tablespoons thyme, chopped	✓ 2 tablespoons basil, minced ✓ 2 cloves garlic, minced ✓ 1 ¼ tablespoons sea salt ✓ 2 tablespoons xanthan gum ✓ ½ cup millet flour ✓ 1 cup potato starch, not flour ✓ 1 cup sorghum flour Gluten-free cornmeal for dusting
❖ For 5 minutes, turn on the oven and then turn it off, keeping the oven door closed. In a small bowl, mix warm water and a pinch of sugar. Add the yeast and stir gently. ❖ Leave for 7 minutes. In a large bowl, whisk herbs, garlic, salt, xanthan gum, starch and flours well. Once the yeast has proofed, pour into the bowl of flours.	❖ Whisk in the egg, lemon juice, honey and olive oil. Mix thoroughly and place in a well greased square baking dish, dusted with cornmeal. ❖ Top with fresh garlic, other herbs and sliced tomatoes. Place in the heated oven and let rise for half an hour. Turn on the oven to 375oF and after preheating leave it for 20 minutes. ❖ The flatbread is ready when the tops are lightly browned. Remove from oven and pan immediately and let cool. Best served when warm.

27) MEDITERRANEAN STYLE HALIBUT SANDWICHES

Preparation Time: 23 minutes	Cooking Time:	Servings: 4

✓ 2 full cups arugula or 2 oz. grated zest of 1 large lemon ✓ 1 tablespoon capers, drained and crushed ✓ 2 tablespoons fresh flat-leaf parsley, chopped ✓ ¼ cup fresh basil, chopped ✓ ¼ cup sun-dried tomatoes, chopped ✓ ¼ cup reduced-fat mayonnaise	✓ 1 garlic clove, cut in half 1 ✓ 14-ounce piece of ciabatta bread with ends cut and split in half, horizontally ✓ 2 tablespoons plus ✓ 1 teaspoon olive oil, divided Kosher salt and freshly ground pepper 2 pieces or 6-ounce halibut fillets, skinned ✓ Cooking spray
❖ Heat oven to 450oF. Using cooking spray, coat a baking sheet. Season the halibut with a pinch of pepper and salt plus rub with a tablespoon of oil and arrange on the baking sheet. ❖ Then place in the oven and bake until cooked through or for ten to fifteen minutes. Remove from oven and let cool. Take a slice of bread and coat sliced portions with olive oil.	❖ Place in the oven and bake until golden brown, about six to eight minutes. Remove from heat and rub garlic over bread. Combine in a medium bowl: lemon zest, capers, parsley, basil, sun-dried tomatoes and mayonnaise. ❖ Then add the halibut, mashing with a fork until flaky. Spread the mixture on one side of the bread, add the arugula and cover with the other half of the bread and serve.

28) EGG AND BACON SANDWICH OPEN FACE

Preparation Time: 20 minutes	Cooking Time:	Servings: 1

✓ ¼ oz low-fat cheddar, shredded ✓ ½ small jalapeno, thinly sliced ✓ ½ whole wheat English muffin, split ✓ 1 large organic egg 1 thick slice of tomato	✓ 1 piece of turkey bacon ✓ 2 thin slices of red onion ✓ 4-5 sprigs of fresh cilantro ✓ Cooking spray Pepper to taste
Directions: ❖ Over medium heat, place a skillet, cook bacon until crispy and set aside. ❖ In the same skillet, drain oils, and place ½ English muffin and heat for at least one minute per side.	❖ Transfer the muffin to a serving plate. Coat the same skillet with cooking spray and fry the egg to desired degree of doneness. ❖ Once cooked, place the egg on top of the muffin. Add cilantro, tomato, onion, jalapeno and bacon on top of the egg. ❖ Serve and enjoy.

29) PIZZA WITH COCONUT FLOUR

Preparation Time: 35 minutes	Cooking Time:	Servings: 4

✓ 2 tablespoons psyllium husk powder ✓ ¾ cup coconut flour ✓ 1 teaspoon garlic powder ✓ ½ teaspoon salt ✓ ½ teaspoon baking soda ✓ 1 cup boiling water	✓ 1 teaspoon apple cider vinegar ✓ 3 eggs Toppings ✓ 3 tablespoons tomato sauce ✓ 1½ oz. mozzarella cheese ✓ 1 tablespoon basil, freshly chopped
❖ Preheat oven to 350 degrees F and grease a baking sheet. ❖ Mix the coconut flour, salt, psyllium husk powder, and garlic powder until fully combined	❖ Add the eggs, apple cider vinegar and baking soda and mix with boiling water. ❖ Place the dough on a baking sheet and cover with the toppings. Transfer to the oven and bake for about 20 minutes. Unmold and serve warm.

30) KETO PEPPERONI PIZZA

Preparation Time: 40 minutes	**Cooking Time**:	**Servings: 4**

Ingredients:	Ingredients:
✓ Crust 6 oz. mozzarella, shredded ✓ 4 eggs Garnish ✓ 1 teaspoon dried oregano	✓ 1½ oz. bell bell pepper ✓ 3 tablespoons tomato paste ✓ 5 oz. mozzarella, shredded Olives
❖ Preheat oven to 400 degrees F and grease a baking sheet. ❖ Whisk together eggs and cheese in a bowl and spread on baking sheet. ❖ Transfer to oven and bake for about 15 minutes until golden brown.	❖ Remove from oven and allow to cool. Increase oven temperature to 450 degrees F. ❖ Spread tomato paste on crust and add oregano, peppers, cheese and olives. Bake for an additional 10 minutes and serve warm.

31) PIZZA WITH BASIL AND FRESH PEPPERS

Preparation Time: 25 minutes	**Cooking Time**:	**Servings: 3**

Ingredients:	Ingredients:
Pizza base ✓ ½ cup almond flour ✓ 2 tablespoons cream cheese ✓ 1 teaspoon Italian seasoning ✓ ½ teaspoon black pepper ✓ 6 ounces mozzarella cheese ✓ 2 tablespoons psyllium husk ✓ 2 tablespoons fresh Parmesan cheese	✓ 1 large egg ✓ ½ teaspoon salt ✓ Condiments ✓ 4 ounces cheddar cheese, shredded ✓ ¼ cup marinara sauce ✓ 2/3 cup medium bell bell pepper ✓ 1 medium vine tomato ✓ 3 tablespoons basil, freshly chopped
Directions: ❖ Preheat oven to 400 degrees F and grease a baking sheet. ❖ Microwave the mozzarella cheese for about 30 seconds and add the remaining pizza crust. ❖ Add the remaining pizza ingredients to the cheese and mix together.	❖ Flatten the dough and transfer to the oven. Bake for about 10 minutes and remove the pizza from the oven. ❖ Top the pizza with the toppings and bake for another 10 minutes. ❖ Remove the pizza from the oven and allow it to cool.

32) PIZZA WITH BASIL AND ARTICHOKES

Preparation Time: 1 hour and 20 minutes	Cooking Time:	Servings: 4

Ingredients:

- ✓ 1 cup canned passata
- ✓ 2 cups flour
- ✓ 1 cup warm water
- ✓ 1 pinch sugar
- ✓ 1 teaspoon active dry yeast
- ✓ ¾ teaspoon salt
- ✓ 2 tablespoons olive oil

Ingredients:

- ✓ 1 ½ cups frozen artichoke hearts
- ✓ ¼ cup grated Asiago cheese
- ✓ ½ onion, chopped
- ✓ 3 cloves garlic, chopped
- ✓ 1 tablespoon dried oregano
- ✓ 1 cup dried tomatoes, chopped
- ✓ ½ teaspoon red pepper
- ✓ 5-6 basil leaves, torn

Directions:

- ❖ Sift the flour and salt into a bowl and stir in the yeast. Mix the warm water, olive oil and sugar in another bowl.
- ❖ Add the wet mixture to the dry mixture and beat until you have a soft dough. Place the dough on a lightly floured work surface and knead it well for 4-5 minutes until it is elastic.
- ❖ Transfer the dough to a greased bowl. Cover with plastic wrap and let rise for 50-60 minutes in a warm place until doubled in size. Roll out the dough to a thickness of about 12 inches.

- ❖ Preheat oven to 400 F. Heat the oil in a saucepan over medium heat and sauté the onion and garlic for 3-4 minutes.
- ❖ Add the tomatoes and oregano and bring to a boil. Decrease the heat and simmer for another 5 minutes.
- ❖ Transfer the pizza crust to a baking sheet. Spread the sauce over the entire surface and add the artichoke hearts and sun-dried tomatoes.
- ❖ Scatter the cheese and bake for 15 minutes until golden brown. Add red pepper flakes and basil leaves and serve in slices.

33) SPANISH STYLE JAMON PIZZA

Preparation Time: 45 minutes	Cooking Time:	Servings: 4

Ingredients:

- ✓ 2 cups flour
- ✓ 1 cup lukewarm water
- ✓ 1 pinch sugar
- ✓ 1 teaspoon active dry yeast
- ✓ ¾ teaspoon salt

Ingredients:

- ✓ 2 tablespoons olive oil
- ✓ ½ cup tomato sauce
- ✓ ½ cup sliced mozzarella cheese
- ✓ 4 oz jamon serrano, sliced
- ✓ 7 fresh basil leaves

Directions:

- ❖ Sift the flour and salt into a bowl and stir in the yeast. Mix the warm water, olive oil and sugar in another bowl.
- ❖ Add the wet mixture to the dry mixture and beat until you have a soft dough.
- ❖ Place the dough on a lightly floured work surface and knead it thoroughly for 4-5 minutes until it is elastic. Transfer the dough to a greased bowl.

- ❖ Cover with plastic wrap and let rise for 50-60 minutes in a warm place until doubled in size.
- ❖ Roll out the dough to a thickness of about 12 inches. Preheat the oven to 400 F.
- ❖ Line a pizza pan with baking paper. Spread the tomato sauce over the crust. Arrange the mozzarella slices on top of the sauce and then the jamon serrano.
- ❖ Bake for 15 minutes or until the cheese melts.
- ❖ Remove from oven and top with basil. Cut into slices and serve warm.

34) ITALIAN MUSHROOM PIZZA

Preparation Time: 45 minutes	Cooking Time:	Servings: 4

For the crust
- ✓ 2 cups flour
- ✓ 1 cup warm water
- ✓ 1 pinch sugar
- ✓ 1 teaspoon active dry yeast
- ✓ ¾ teaspoon salt
- ✓ 2 tablespoons olive oil

For the dressing
- ✓ 1 tablespoon olive oil
- ✓ 2 medium cremini mushrooms, sliced
- ✓ 1 clove of garlic, minced

- ✓ ½ cup unsweetened tomato sauce
- ✓ 1 teaspoon sugar
- ✓ 1 bay leaf
- ✓ 1 teaspoon dried oregano
- ✓ 1 teaspoon dried basil Salt and black pepper to taste
- ✓ ½ cup grated mozzarella cheese
- ✓ ½ cup grated Parmesan cheese
- ✓ 6 black olives, pitted and chopped

❖ Sift the flour and salt into a bowl and stir in the yeast. Mix the warm water, olive oil and sugar in another bowl.
❖ Add the wet mixture to the dry mixture and beat until you have a soft dough. Place the dough on a lightly floured work surface and knead it well for 4-5 minutes until it is elastic.
❖ Transfer the dough to a greased bowl. Cover with plastic wrap and let rise for 50-60 minutes in a warm place until doubled in size.
❖ Roll out the dough to a thickness of about 12 inches.

❖ Preheat the oven to 400 F. Line a pizza pan with baking paper.
❖ Heat the olive oil in a medium skillet and sauté the mushrooms until softened, 5 minutes. Stir in the garlic and cook until fragrant, 30 seconds.
❖ Add the tomato sauce, sugar, bay leaf, oregano, basil, salt and black pepper.
❖ Cook for 2 minutes and turn off the heat. Spread the sauce over the crust, top with the mozzarella and parmesan cheese and then the olives.
❖ Bake until the cheeses are melted, 15 minutes. Remove pizza, cut into slices and serve warm.

35) CHICKEN BACON RANCH PIZZA

Preparation Time: 45 minutes	Cooking Time:	Servings: 4

For the crust

- ✓ 2 cups flour
- ✓ 1 cup lukewarm water
- ✓ 1 pinch sugar
- ✓ 1 teaspoon active dry yeast
- ✓ ¾ teaspoon salt
- ✓ 2 tablespoons olive oil
- ✓

For the ranch dressing
- ✓ 1 tablespoon butter
- ✓ 2 cloves garlic, minced
- ✓ 1 tablespoon cream cheese
- ✓ ¼ cup half-and-half
- ✓ 1 tablespoon dry Ranch seasoning mix
- ✓ 3 slices bacon, minced
- ✓ 2 chicken breasts
- ✓ Salt and black pepper to taste
- ✓ 1 cup grated mozzarella cheese
- ✓ 6 leaves fresh basil

❖ Sift the flour and salt into a bowl and stir in the yeast. Mix the warm water, olive oil and sugar in another bowl.
❖ Add the wet mixture to the dry mixture and beat until you have a soft dough.
❖ Place the dough on a lightly floured work surface and knead it thoroughly for 4-5 minutes until it is elastic. Transfer the dough to a greased bowl.
❖ Cover with plastic wrap and let rise for 50-60 minutes in a warm place until doubled in size. Roll out the dough to a thickness of about 12 inches.

❖ Preheat the oven to 400 F. Line a pizza pan with baking paper. In a bowl, mix the sauce ingredients: butter, garlic, cream cheese, half-and-half, and ranch mixture. Set aside. Heat a grill pan over medium heat and cook bacon until crisp and brown, 5 minutes. Transfer to a plate and set aside. Season chicken with salt and pepper and grill in skillet on both sides until golden brown, 10 minutes. Remove to a plate, let cool, and cut into thin slices. Spread ranch dressing on pizza crust, followed by chicken and bacon, then mozzarella and basil. Bake for 5 minutes or until the cheese melts. Cut into slices and serve warm.

36) BAKED AUTUMN VEGETABLES WITH RIGATONI

Preparation Time: 45 minutes	Cooking Time:	Servings: 6

Ingredients:	Ingredients:
<ul><li>1 pound squash, chopped</li><li>1 zucchini, chopped</li><li>2 tablespoons grated Pecorino-Romano cheese</li><li>1 onion, chopped</li></ul>	<ul><li>1 pound rigatoni</li><li>2 tablespoons olive oil Salt and black pepper to taste</li><li>½ teaspoon garlic powder</li><li>½ cup dry white wine</li></ul>

Directions:

❖ Preheat oven to 420 F. Combine zucchini, squash, onion and olive oil in a bowl. Arrange on a foil lined baking sheet and season with salt, pepper and garlic powder.

❖ Bake for 30 minutes until tender. In a pot of boiling water, cook rigatoni for 8-10 minutes until al dente.

❖ Drain and set aside. In a food processor, place ½ cup of the roasted vegetables and the wine and pulse until smooth.

❖ Transfer to a skillet over medium heat. Stir in rigatoni and cook until heated through. Add remaining roasted vegetables and pecorino cheese to serve.

37) PASTA WITH WALNUT PESTO

Preparation Time: 10 minutes	Cooking Time:	Servings: 4

Ingredients:	Ingredients:
<ul><li>8 ounces whole-wheat pasta</li><li>¼ cup walnuts, chopped</li><li>3 cloves garlic, finely chopped</li></ul>	<ul><li>½ cup fresh dill, chopped</li><li>¼ cup grated Parmesan cheese 3 tablespoons extra-virgin olive oil</li></ul>

❖ Cook whole wheat pasta according to package instructions, drain and let cool.

❖ Place the olive oil, dill, garlic, Parmesan cheese and walnuts in a food processor and blend for 15 seconds or until a paste forms.

❖ Pour over the cooled pasta and stir. Serve immediately.

38) BEEF CARBONARA

Preparation Time: 30 minutes	Cooking Time:	Servings: 4

Ingredients:	Ingredients:
<ul><li>16 ounces linguine</li><li>4 slices bacon, chopped</li><li>1 ¼ cups whipping cream.</li></ul>	<ul><li>¼ cup mayonnaise Salt and black pepper to taste</li><li>4 egg yolks</li><li>1 cup grated Parmesan cheese</li></ul>

❖ In a pot of boiling water, cook linguine for 8-10 minutes until al dente. Drain and set aside.

❖ Add bacon to a skillet and cook over medium heat until crispy, 5 minutes. Set aside. Pour heavy cream into a saucepan and let simmer for 5 minutes. Whisk in mayonnaise and season with salt and pepper.

❖ Cook for 1 minute and pour 2 tablespoons of the mixture into a medium bowl. Allow to cool and stir in the egg yolks. Pour the mixture into the pot and stir quickly.

❖ Stir in the Parmesan cheese and add the pasta. Garnish with more Parmesan cheese. Cook for 1 minute to warm the pasta.

39) TUSCAN STYLE CHICKEN LINGUINE

Preparation Time: 35 minutes	**Cooking Time**:	**Servings**: 4

✓ 16 ounces linguine ✓ 2 tablespoons olive oil ✓ 4 chicken breasts ✓ 1 medium white onion, chopped ✓ 1 cup sun-dried tomatoes in oil, chopped ✓ 1 red bell bell pepper, seeded and chopped	✓ 5 cloves garlic, chopped ✓ ¾ cup chicken broth ✓ 1 ½ cups heavy cream ✓ ¾ cup grated pecorino romano cheese ✓ 1 cup sprouts, chopped Salt and black pepper to taste
❖ In a pot of boiling water, cook linguine for 8-10 minutes until al dente. Drain and set aside. Heat the olive oil in a large skillet, season the chicken with salt and black pepper and cook in the oil until golden brown on the outside and cooked through on the inside, 7 to 8 minutes. ❖ Transfer chicken to a plate and cut into 4 slices each. Set aside. Add onion, sun-dried tomatoes, and bell bell pepper to skillet and sauté until softened, 5 minutes.	❖ Add garlic and cook until fragrant, 1 minute. Deglaze the skillet with the chicken broth and stir in the heavy cream. Simmer for 2 minutes and stir in pecorino romano cheese until melted, 2 minutes. ❖ Once the cheese has melted, stir in the kale to wilt it and adjust the flavor with salt and black pepper. Stir in the linguine and chicken until well coated in the sauce. Unmold and serve warm.

40) CLASSIC BEEF LASAGNA

Preparation Time: 70 minutes	**Cooking Time**:	**Servings**: 4

✓ 1 pound lasagna ✓ 2 tablespoons olive oil ✓ 1 pound ground beef ✓ 1 medium white onion, chopped	✓ 1 teaspoon Italian seasoning Salt and black pepper to taste ✓ 1 cup marinara sauce ✓ ½ cup grated Parmesan cheese
❖ Preheat the oven to 350 F. Heat the olive oil in a skillet and add the beef and onion. Cook until beef is brown, 7-8 minutes. Season with Italian seasoning, salt and pepper. ❖ Cook for 1 minute and stir in marinara sauce. Simmer for 3 minutes. Spread a layer of the beef mixture in a lightly greased baking dish and make a first single layer over the beef mixture. Top with a single layer of lasagna sheets.	❖ Repeat layering two more times using the remaining ingredients in the same amounts. Sprinkle with the parmesan cheese. Bake until cheese melts and bubbles with sauce, 20 minutes. ❖ Remove lasagna, let cool for 2 minutes and arrange on serving plates. Serve warm.

41) BAKED VEGETARIAN SPICY PASTA

Preparation Time: 45 minutes	**Cooking Time**:	**Servings**: 4

✓ 16 ounces penne pasta ✓ 1 tablespoon olive oil ✓ 1 cup chopped mixed peppers ✓ 1 chopped yellow squash ✓ 1 red onion cut in half and sliced ✓ 1 cup sliced white mushrooms Salt and black pepper to taste	✓ ¼ teaspoon red pepper flakes ✓ 1 cup marinara sauce ✓ 1 cup grated mozzarella cheese ✓ 1 cup grated Parmesan cheese ✓ ¼ cup chopped fresh basil
❖ In a pot of boiling water, cook penne for 8-10 minutes until al dente. Drain and set aside. Heat the olive oil in a cast iron and sauté the peppers, squash, onion and mushrooms. Cook until softened, 5 minutes. Add garlic and cook until fragrant, 30 seconds. Season with salt, pepper and red pepper flakes. Add the marinara sauce and cook for 5 minutes.	❖ Stir in penne and spread mozzarella cheese and Parmesan cheese. Bake until cheeses are melted and golden brown on top, 15 minutes. ❖ Let cool for 2 minutes and serve on serving plates. Serve warm.

42) SPAGHETTI WITH PARMESAN CHEESE IN MUSHROOM AND TOMATO SAUCE

Preparation Time: 30 minutes	Cooking Time:	Servings: 4

Ingredients:

- ✓ 16 ounces spaghetti, cut in half
- ✓ 2 cups mushrooms, chopped
- ✓ 1 bell bell pepper, chopped
- ✓ ½ cup yellow onion, chopped
- ✓ 3 cloves garlic, chopped
- ✓ ½ teaspoon five-spice powder

Ingredients:

- ✓ 4 tablespoons fresh parsley, chopped
- ✓ 1 tablespoon tomato paste
- ✓ 2 ripe tomatoes, chopped
- ✓ ½ cup Parmesan cheese, grated
- ✓ ¼ cup olive oil Salt and black pepper to taste

Directions:

- ❖ Heat the olive oil in a skillet over medium heat. Add mushrooms, bell bell pepper, onion and garlic and sauté for 4-5 minutes until tender.
- ❖ Add salt, black pepper, 2 tablespoons parsley, five-spice powder, tomato paste and tomatoes; mix well and cook for 10-12 minutes. In a pot of boiling salted water, add pasta and cook until al dente, about 8-10 minutes, stirring occasionally.

- ❖ Drain and stir into the vegetable mixture. Serve topped with Parmesan cheese and the remaining fresh parsley.

43) CHICKEN FARFALLE WITH MUSTARD

Preparation Time: 40 minutes	Cooking Time:	Servings: 4

Ingredients:

- ✓ 16 ounces of farfalle
- ✓ 1 tablespoon olive oil
- ✓ 4 chicken breasts cut into strips Salt and black pepper to taste
- ✓ 1 finely sliced yellow onion
- ✓ 1 sliced yellow bell bell pepper

Ingredients:

- ✓ 1 clove of minced garlic
- ✓ 1 tablespoon whole grain mustard
- ✓ 5 tablespoons heavy cream
- ✓ 1 cup chopped green mustard
- ✓ 1 tablespoon chopped parsley

Directions:

- ❖ In a pot of boiling water, cook farfalle for 8-10 minutes until al dente. Drain and set aside. Heat olive oil in a large skillet, season chicken with salt, black pepper and cook in oil until golden brown, 10 minutes. Set aside.
- ❖ Stir in onion, bell bell pepper and cook until softened, 5 minutes. Combine garlic and cook until fragrant, 30 seconds.

- ❖ Stir in mustard and heavy cream; simmer 2 minutes and stir in chicken and mustard. Allow to wilt for 2 minutes and adjust taste with salt and black pepper.
- ❖ Add the farfalle, let it warm for 1 minute, and arrange on serving plates. Garnish with the parsley and serve hot.

Chapter 3. DINNER

44) MOROCCAN LAMB PIE

Preparation Time: 20 minutes	**Cooking Time**: 1 hour	**Servings**: 8

✓ 2 tablespoons of olive oil ✓ 1 medium onion, chopped (about 1¼ cups) ✓ 3 carrots, finely chopped (about 1 cup) ✓ 1 teaspoon ground turmeric ✓ 2 garlic cloves, minced ✓ 1 pound (454 g) ground lamb ✓ ⅓ cup of golden raisins	✓ ½ cup of toasted pistachios ✓ ¼ cup chopped fresh cilantro ✓ 1 teaspoon ground cinnamon ✓ 6 eggs ✓ 1 (5-ounce / 142-g) container of 2% Greek yogurt ✓ Olive oil spray or other non-stick spray ✓ 12 sheets of frozen phyllo dough, thawed
❖ Preheat the oven to 375ºF (190ºC). ❖ In a large skillet, heat 1 tablespoon olive oil over medium heat. Add onion and carrots and cook, stirring occasionally for 5-6 minutes, until onion is translucent. Add turmeric and garlic; cook for 1 minute. Add remaining 1 tablespoon olive oil and ground lamb to skillet. Cook, breaking up the meat with a wooden spoon as it cooks, for 6 to 8 minutes, until the lamb is browned. ❖ Stir in raisins, pistachios, cilantro and cinnamon until well combined; set aside. ❖ In a medium bowl, whisk together eggs and yogurt; set aside.	❖ Spray a 9-inch baking dish with olive oil or other cooking spray. On a clean work surface, stack 4 sheets of phyllo, spray both sides with cooking spray and place them in the stack in the prepared baking dish, extending the edges of the stack over the sides of the baking dish. Repeat with a second stack of 4 phyllo sheets; place them crosswise on top of the first stack, extending the edges over the top edge of the pan. ❖ Fill phyllo crust with lamb mixture, then pour in egg mixture. Spray the remaining 4 sheets of phyllo with cooking spray and cut them in half. Place them on top of the filling to cover it completely. Fold phyllo toward center over filling. Spray with more cooking spray. ❖ Bake for 45-50 minutes, until golden brown. Allow to rest for 15 minutes before serving.

45) LEMON AND DILL TILAPIA

Preparation Time: 5 minutes	**Cooking Time**: 20 minutes	**Servings**: 4

✓ 4 (4-ounce / 113-g) tilapia fillets ✓ ¼ teaspoon salt ✓ ½ teaspoon of freshly ground black pepper	✓ 2 tablespoons unsalted butter ✓ 2 large lemons, 1 squeezed and 1 sliced ✓ ¼ cup chopped fresh dill
❖ Preheat the oven to 350ºF (180ºC). ❖ Place tilapia fillets in a glass baking dish. Season with the salt and pepper.	❖ Top each fillet with ½ tablespoon butter, the lemon juice and 1 tablespoon dill. Once they are coated, place the lemon slices on top. ❖ Bake for 15-20 minutes, or until fish flakes with a fork. Divide among 4 containers for storage.

46) BAKED TILAPIA WITH PISTACHIO CRUST

Preparation Time: 10 minutes	**Cooking Time**: 15 minutes	**Servings**: 4

✓ 4 (4-ounce / 113-g) tilapia fillets ✓ ¼ teaspoon salt ✓ ½ teaspoon of freshly ground black pepper ✓ ½ teaspoon of garlic powder ✓ ¼ cup low-fat Greek yogurt	✓ ½ cup dry unseasoned breadcrumbs ✓ ½ cup finely chopped raw pistachios ✓ 1 teaspoon of dried oregano ✓ 1 teaspoon of dried thyme ✓ Non-stick cooking spray
❖ Preheat oven to 375ºF (190ºC). Cover a baking sheet with aluminum foil and coat with nonstick cooking spray. ❖ Season fillets with salt, pepper and garlic powder. Spread 1 tablespoon yogurt over each fillet until evenly coated. Set aside.	❖ In a shallow dish, mix together the bread crumbs, pistachios, oregano and thyme. Press each fillet into the pistachio and breadcrumb mixture on both sides until well coated. ❖ Place fillets on prepared baking sheet and bake for 12-15 minutes, or until cooked through. Divide among 4 containers for storage.

47) GARLIC AND LEMON TILAPIA WITH VEGETABLES

Preparation Time: 5 minutes	**Cooking Time:** 15 minutes	**Servings: 4**

Ingredients:

- ✓
- ✓ 3 cups of broccoli florets
- ✓ 1 cup sliced yellow squash (about 1 medium)
- ✓ 2 tablespoons plus 2 teaspoons of extra virgin olive oil, divided
- ✓ Salt and freshly ground black pepper, to taste
- ✓ 2 tablespoons fresh lemon juice
- ✓ 2 tablespoons chopped shallot

Ingredients:

- ✓ 2 tablespoons of chopped fresh parsley
- ✓ 1 tablespoon chopped garlic
- ✓ 4 tilapia fillets (4 ounces / 113 g each)
- ✓ 5 ounces (142 g) arugula
- ✓ 2 spoons of grated parmesan cheese

Directions:

- ❖ Preheat the oven to 400°F (205°C). Coat a baking sheet with cooking spray.
- ❖ Place broccoli and squash on baking sheet, drizzle with 1 tablespoon olive oil and season with salt and pepper, if desired. Push the vegetables to the sides of the baking dish.
- ❖ In a small bowl, stir together 1 tablespoon olive oil, the lemon juice, shallot, parsley, garlic, ¼ teaspoon pepper and ⅛ teaspoon salt. Place the tilapia fillets on the baking sheet between the vegetables and drizzle with the lemon mixture, gently pressing the fish down, turning and seasoning the other side.

- ❖ Transfer the pan to the oven and bake until the fish flakes easily with a fork, 12 to 15 minutes.
- ❖ Meanwhile, in a medium bowl, mix the arugula, remaining 2 teaspoons olive oil, Parmesan cheese, and salt and pepper, if desired. Stir to combine.
- ❖ Place a tilapia fillet on each of the 4 plates. Spread the roasted vegetables and arugula salad on the plates.

---

48) SLICES OF TUNA IN SESAME CRUST BLANCHED

Preparation Time: 5 minutes	**Cooking Time:** 6 minutes	**Servings: 4**

Ingredients:

- ✓ 2 tablespoons low-sodium soy sauce
- ✓ 1 tablespoon of sesame oil
- ✓ 1 tablespoon of rice vinegar
- ✓ ½ tablespoon of honey
- ✓ 4 (4-ounce / 113-g) ahi tuna steaks

Ingredients:

- ✓ ¼ cup white sesame seeds
- ✓ ¼ cup black sesame seeds
- ✓ 1 tablespoon of extra virgin olive oil
- ✓ 2 shallots, chopped

Directions:

- ❖ In a small bowl, mix together the soy sauce, sesame oil, vinegar and honey.
- ❖ Coat the tuna steaks with the mixture.

- ❖ Spread the black and white sesame seeds on a plate and press both sides of each tuna steak into the seeds to coat them.
- ❖ In a nonstick skillet or pan, heat the olive oil over high heat. Cook the tuna steaks for 30-45 seconds on each side. You will know the tuna is done when it has been seared white on the outside but remains pink in the center. Divide among 4 containers. Add the shallots.

49) HALIBUT WITH BEAN AND MANGO SAUCE

Preparation Time: 15 minutes	Cooking Time: 10 minutes	Servings: 4

✓ 1 (15-ounce / 425-g) can no salt added black beans, drained and rinsed ✓ 1 (15-ounce / 425-g) can of diced mango with juice, drained ✓ ½ medium red onion, chopped ✓ ½ medium red bell pepper, diced ✓ 3 tablespoons fresh coriander chopped ✓ Juice of 1 large lime	✓ Juice of 1 large lemon ✓ 3 tablespoons of extra virgin olive oil ✓ 1 teaspoon of freshly ground black pepper ✓ 1 garlic clove, minced ✓ 4 (4-ounce / 113-g) halibut fillets
❖ Preheat grill to medium-high heat. In a large bowl, mix together the beans, mango, onion, bell bell pepper, cilantro and lime juice. Divide among 4 containers. ❖ In a small bowl, mix together the lemon juice, oil, black pepper and garlic.	❖ Coat the halibut fillets in the lemon marinade and let stand for 10 minutes. Grill for 2 minutes on each side. Remove from grill and allow to rest. Divide among 4 containers for storage. ❖ To serve, reheat and top each fillet with a generous portion of the sauce.

50) BAKED SALMON JERK

Preparation Time: 5 minutes	Cooking Time: 12-15 minutes	Servings: 4

✓ 2 tablespoons of extra virgin olive oil, divided ✓ 2½ teaspoons of dried thyme ✓ 2 teaspoons of ground allspice ✓ 2 teaspoons of onion powder	✓ 2 teaspoons of freshly ground black pepper ✓ ½ teaspoon ground cinnamon ✓ ½ teaspoon of cayenne pepper ✓ 4 (4-ounce / 113-g) salmon fillets with skin
❖ Preheat oven to 350ºF (180ºC). Lightly coat a baking sheet with ½ tablespoon oil. ❖ In a small bowl, stir together the thyme, allspice, onion powder, black pepper, cinnamon and cayenne pepper. Lightly coat the salmon fillets with the remaining 1½ tablespoons oil and drizzle with the rub.	❖ Place the salmon, skin side down, on the prepared baking sheet. Bake for 12-15 minutes, or until salmon is cooked through and flakes easily with a fork. Divide among 4 containers for storage.

51) ROASTED AND BLACKENED SALMON WITH ASPARAGUS

Preparation Time: 10 minutes	Cooking Time: 15 minutes	Servings: 4

✓ 2 teaspoons of dried parsley ✓ 1 teaspoon of ground cumin ✓ 1 teaspoon garlic powder ✓ 1 teaspoon of onion powder ✓ 1 teaspoon of sweet paprika ✓ 1 teaspoon dark brown sugar ✓ ¼ teaspoon of chili powder	✓ ¼ teaspoon salt, or more to taste ✓ ¼ teaspoon freshly ground black pepper, or more to taste ✓ 4 skinless salmon fillets (6 oz / 170 g each) ✓ 1 pound (454 g) asparagus, hard ends cut off ✓ 1 tablespoon of extra virgin olive oil ✓ 1 lemon, cut in four
❖ Preheat the oven to 425ºF (220ºC). Line two large baking sheets with aluminum foil and lightly spray with cooking spray. ❖ In a shallow bowl, combine the parsley, cumin, garlic powder, onion powder, paprika, brown sugar, chili powder and ¼ teaspoon salt and black pepper and mix the blackened seasoning well. ❖ Place salmon on a plate and coat with cooking spray. Season with 1 teaspoon of the blackened seasoning, turn, coat with more cooking spray and season with another teaspoon of seasoning. Arrange on one of the prepared baking sheets.	❖ Place asparagus in a small bowl and drizzle with olive oil and sprinkle with salt and pepper, if desired. Arrange on the second prepared baking sheet. ❖ Transfer the salmon and asparagus to the oven and roast until the asparagus is tender and lightly browned and the salmon flakes easily with a fork, is blackened and crispy on the outside and an instant-read thermometer reads 145ºF (63ºC), 12 to 15 minutes, depending on the thickness of the salmon and asparagus. ❖ Portion onto 4 plates and squeeze fresh lemon juice over each.

52) PACKETS OF ORANGE SALMON

Preparation Time: 15 minutes	**Cooking Time:** 20 minutes	**Servings: 4**

Ingredients:

- ✓ Juice of 1 lemon
- ✓ 1 tablespoon of extra virgin olive oil
- ✓ 2 teaspoons of dried thyme
- ✓ ¼ teaspoon salt
- ✓ ¼ teaspoon freshly ground black pepper
- ✓ 2 cups sliced yellow summer squash (about 2 medium)

Ingredients:

- ✓ 2 cups sliced zucchini (about 2 medium)
- ✓ 1 small red onion, thinly sliced
- ✓ 2 blood oranges, peeled and thinly sliced
- ✓ 4 skinless salmon fillets (6 oz / 170 g each)
- ✓ 4 sprigs of fresh thyme

Directions:

- ❖ Preheat oven to 400°F (205°C). Tear 4 pieces of foil or parchment paper 2 inches longer than the salmon fillets.
- ❖ In a medium bowl, combine the lemon juice, olive oil, dried thyme, salt and pepper.
- ❖ Place the pieces of foil/parchment paper on your work surface and on one side of each piece of foil/parchment paper, place a quarter of the yellow squash, zucchini, red onion and blood orange. Top each vegetable stack with a salmon fillet and drizzle each stack with the lemon juice mixture. Place a sprig of thyme on top of each piece of fish.

- ❖ Fold the other half of the foil/parchment over the ingredients. To seal the packets, start at one corner and tightly fold the edges over about ½ inch all around, overlapping the folds. The foil/parchment should not unravel.
- ❖ Place packets on a baking sheet. Transfer to oven and bake until salmon turns opaque, about 20 minutes.
- ❖ Serve the pouches on a plate or remove the contents to a platter, paying close attention to the steam that escapes when opening because it will be very hot. Pour any liquid left in the foil over the salmon and vegetables.

53) FISH TACOS WITH COLESLAW

Preparation Time: 10 minutes	**Cooking Time:** 5 minutes	**Servings: 2**

Ingredients:

- ✓ 1 teaspoon of ground cumin
- ✓ ½ teaspoon of chili powder
- ✓ ⅛ teaspoon of salt
- ✓ ⅛ teaspoon of freshly ground black pepper
- ✓ 8 ounces (227 g) skinless haddock fillets, cut into 1-inch pieces
- ✓ 2 cups of angel hair cabbage

Ingredients:

- ✓ ½ avocado, chopped
- ✓ 2 tablespoons fresh lime juice
- ✓ 3 teaspoons of extra virgin olive oil
- ✓ 2 (6 inch) whole wheat tortillas, heated
- ✓ Fresh cilantro, for serving

Directions:

- ❖ In a small bowl, combine the cumin, chili powder, salt and pepper. Add the haddock and stir to coat.
- ❖ In a separate small bowl, mix together the kale, avocado, lime juice and 1 teaspoon olive oil.

- ❖ In a medium skillet, heat the remaining 2 teaspoons olive oil over medium-high heat. Add the haddock and cook, turning, until the fish is just opaque and flakes easily with a fork, 4 to 5 minutes.
- ❖ Divide fish among warmed tortillas and top with cabbage and avocado mixture. Serve garnished with fresh cilantro.

54) ROAST FILLET WITH CANNELLINI BEANS

Preparation Time: 5 minutes	**Cooking Time**: 30 minutes	**Servings: 4**

Ingredients:

- ✓ 2 (15-ounce / 425-g) cans of cannellini beans or other white beans, rinsed and drained
- ✓ 1 medium red onion, sliced
- ✓ 1 large red bell pepper, sliced
- ✓ 1 pint cherry tomatoes, halved (a pint of mixed colors provides a striking dish)
- ✓ 4 garlic cloves, minced
- ✓ 2 teaspoons of dried marjoram

Ingredients:

- ✓ 2 tablespoons of extra virgin olive oil
- ✓ Salt and freshly ground black pepper, to taste
- ✓ ¼ cup white wine
- ✓ 4 plaice fillets (4 oz / 113 g each)
- ✓ 1 lemon, cut in half
- ✓ 4 tablespoons of fresh basil, coarsely chopped

Directions:

- ❖ Preheat the oven to 400°F (205°C). Line a baking sheet with aluminum foil.
- ❖ Spread the beans, onion and bell bell pepper on the baking sheet and arrange the chopped cherry tomatoes on top between them. Sprinkle with half of the minced garlic and all of the marjoram. Drizzle with 1 tablespoon of the olive oil and season with a pinch of salt and black pepper. Transfer to the oven and roast for 10 minutes.

- ❖ Remove the pan from the oven and douse with the white wine. Move the vegetables to the sides and place the flounder on the baking sheet. Sprinkle with the remaining garlic and 1 tablespoon olive oil. Season lightly with salt and pepper, if desired, and squeeze the lemon over the top. Roast until the fish is cooked through, opaque and flakes easily with a fork, about 15 minutes.
- ❖ Place a fillet on each of 4 serving plates. Distribute vegetables on plates and sprinkle each serving with 1 tablespoon fresh basil.

55) LEMON COD WITH ROASTED VEGETABLES

Preparation Time: 15 minutes	**Cooking Time**: 25 minutes	**Servings: 4**

Ingredients:

- ✓ 6 medium carrots, sliced
- ✓ 3 cups or about 1 medium head of cauliflower, cut into small florets
- ✓ 3 tablespoons of extra virgin olive oil
- ✓ Salt and freshly ground pepper, to taste
- ✓ 2 cups instant brown rice
- ✓ 1 tablespoon fresh grated ginger

Ingredients:

- ✓ 2 garlic cloves, grated
- ✓ 2 lemons, sliced
- ✓ 4 cod fillets (4 ounces / 113 g each)
- ✓ ½ cup of dry white wine
- ✓ ¼ cup chopped fresh chives, plus more for garnish

Directions:

- ❖ Preheat the oven to 400°F (205°C). Coat a baking sheet with cooking spray.
- ❖ Arrange vegetables on baking sheet and drizzle with 1 tablespoon olive oil and season lightly with salt and pepper, if desired. Bake until tender and golden brown, about 25 minutes.
- ❖ Meanwhile, cook rice according to package directions.
- ❖ In a small bowl, combine 1 tablespoon olive oil, the ginger, garlic, lemon slices, and salt and pepper, if desired. Set aside.

- ❖ In a large skillet, heat the remaining 1 tablespoon olive oil over medium-high heat. When the oil shimmers, add the fish and sauté for 5 minutes, then move it to the side leaving extra room in the pan. Add the ginger/aglic mixture and lemon slices to the skillet and sauté until the lemon slices have turned golden brown, 3 to 4 minutes.
- ❖ Add the white wine and chives and cook until a sauce begins to form, about 3 minutes. Pour some of the sauce over the fish.
- ❖ Add the cooked rice to the pan and simmer until the sauce is fully absorbed, 3 to 5 minutes.
- ❖ Arrange one cod fillet on each of 4 serving plates. Portion the rice and sauce mixture next to the fish. Remove the vegetables from the oven and distribute them on each plate. Garnish with additional chives, if desired.

56) CRISPY COD WITH SWEET POTATO CHIPS

Preparation Time: 20 minutes	**Cooking Time**: 20-30 minutes	**Servings: 5**

Ingredients:

- ✓ 2 large sweet potatoes, cut crosswise into ¼-inch thick rounds
- ✓ 2 tablespoons of extra virgin olive oil, divided
- ✓ 1 tablespoon of fresh rosemary leaves
- ✓ ½ teaspoon salt
- ✓ ¼ teaspoon freshly ground black pepper
- ✓ ¼ cup whole wheat flour
- ✓ 1 large egg

Ingredients:

- ✓ 2 tablespoons of milk 1%
- ✓ ½ cup dry unseasoned breadcrumbs
- ✓ ¼ cup slivered almonds
- ✓ ¼ teaspoon of lemon pepper
- ✓ 1 teaspoon chopped fresh parsley, plus more for serving
- ✓ 5 (4-ounce / 113-g) fresh or frozen cod fillets (thawed)
- ✓ lemon wedges, to serve (optional)

Directions:

- ❖ Place the racks in the upper and lower thirds of the oven and preheat the oven to 450°F (235°C). Line 2 baking sheets with aluminum foil.
- ❖ In a medium bowl, mix the sweet potatoes with 1 tablespoon oil and the rosemary. Season with the salt and pepper. Arrange in an even layer on prepared baking sheet. Bake on top rack, turning once, for 20-30 minutes, or until golden brown.

- ❖ Prepare a dredging station: Place the flour in a small bowl. In a second small bowl, whisk together the egg and milk. In a third, combine the bread crumbs, almonds, lemon pepper and parsley. Coat each cod fillet in the flour, then the egg, then the breadcrumb mixture. Arrange on the second prepared baking sheet and drizzle with the remaining 1 tablespoon oil.
- ❖ Bake the cod on the bottom rack for about 15 minutes, or until crispy and just cooked through.
- ❖ Portion the cod and sweet potatoes into 5 divided containers; fish on one side, chips on the other.
- ❖ To serve, after warming the dish, add the parsley. Serve with lemon wedges (if using).

57) HADDOCK WITH ORANGE AND GINGER

Preparation Time: 10 minutes	**Cooking Time:** 5 minutes	**Servings: 4**

Ingredients:

- ✓ 2 tablespoons of olive oil, divided
- ✓ 1 teaspoon Dijon mustard
- ✓ 2 teaspoons fresh grated ginger
- ✓ 2 teaspoons of honey
- ✓ 1 tablespoon of rice vinegar

Ingredients:

- ✓ 2 teaspoons of low-sodium soy sauce
- ✓ ¼ cup orange juice
- ✓ 4 (6-ounce / 170-g) haddock fillets
- ✓ 1 cup chopped shallots
- ✓ 10 cherry tomatoes, halved

Directions:

- ❖ In a small bowl, combine 1 tablespoon olive oil, mustard, ginger, honey, vinegar, soy sauce and orange juice. Add fish fillets and cover. Allow to marinate in the refrigerator for 1 hour.
- ❖ Heat a large heavy skillet over medium-high heat. Add the remaining olive oil and heat for 1 minute. Add the fish fillets (reserving the marinade), then arrange the scallions and tomato around the edges of the pan. Cook for 1 minute.

- ❖ Turn the fish, lower the heat and pour the marinade over everything. Cook covered for 3 minutes.
- ❖ Serve the haddock with the vegetables and sauce poured over the top

58) CITRUS FLOUNDER IN FOIL		
Preparation Time: 5 minutes	**Cooking Time:** 20 minutes	**Servings: 4**

Ingredients:

- ✓ 4 plaice fillets (6 oz / 170 g)
- ✓ 1 teaspoon of olive oil
- ✓ ½ teaspoon of salt substitute
- ✓ ½ teaspoon of freshly ground pepper
- ✓ 8 thin slices of orange

Ingredients:

- ✓ 8 thin slices of lime
- ✓ 4 sprigs of fresh rosemary
- ✓ Juice of 1 orange
- ✓ Juice of 1 small lime
- ✓ ½ cup of dry white wine

Directions:

- ❖ Preheat the oven to 400°F (205°C).
- ❖ Cut 4 lengths (12 inches) of aluminum foil and arrange them on the counter.
- ❖ Rub each fish fillet with olive oil and season both sides with salt and freshly ground pepper. Place each fillet on aluminum foil. Alternate orange and lime slices on each fillet, assigning 2 of each fruit per fillet.

- ❖ Lay the rosemary sprigs on top of the slices and squeeze the orange and lime juice over each fillet. Pour ¼ of the wine over the first fillet, quickly fold the edges of the foil at the ends, and pull the sides together at the top before rolling a couple of times to seal. Be sure to leave about 3-4 inches of "headroom" for the fish.
- ❖ Repeat with remaining packets and place all 4 packets on a cookie sheet or large baking sheet.
- ❖ Bake for 20 minutes, place each package on a plate, and let your guests cut to the table.

59) POACHED COD IN WINE AND LEMON		
Preparation Time: 5 minutes	**Cooking Time:** 10 minutes	**Servings: 2**

Ingredients:

- ✓ 2 (6-ounce / 170-g) cod fillets
- ✓ Freshly ground black pepper, to taste
- ✓ 1 fresh lemon
- ✓ 1 small fresh tomato, cut into pieces

Ingredients:

- ✓ 4 or 5 sprigs of fresh cilantro, chopped
- ✓ 1 cup of water
- ✓ ½ cup of white wine

Directions:

- ❖ Pat the cod fillets dry with a paper towel and sprinkle generously with black pepper. Cut half the lemon into wedges (for serving) and then squeeze the juice from the other half into a medium-sized casserole dish, large enough to hold the fish fillets.

- ❖ Add the tomato and cilantro to the skillet. Add the water and wine to the skillet and bring to a boil over high heat. Add the cod fillets to the skillet, cover tightly with a lid and remove from heat.
- ❖ Let stand for 10 minutes. Serve with lemon wedges.

60) ASIAN COD FILLETS

Preparation Time: 5 minutes	Cooking Time: 5 minutes	Servings: 2

✓ 3 tablespoons unsweetened orange juice ✓ 2 tablespoons of olive oil ✓ 2 tablespoons of dry mustard ✓ 1 tablespoon of honey ✓ 1 tablespoon of rice vinegar ✓ 2 teaspoons fresh grated ginger	✓ 2 teaspoons of low-sodium soy sauce ✓ 2 (6-ounce / 170-g) cod fillets ✓ Canola oil spray ✓ ½ cup sliced green onions ✓ ½ cup fresh diced tomato
❖ Mix the orange juice, oil, mustard, honey, vinegar, ginger and soy sauce in a non-reactive glass or plastic (not metal) bowl. Add the cod fillets and marinate in the refrigerator, covered, for 45 minutes. ❖ Lightly coat a nonstick skillet with canola oil spray and heat over medium heat. Add the fillets and then nestle the green onions and tomato around the fillets in the skillet. Cook for 1 minute.	❖ Gently turn the fish with a wide spatula and add the rest of the marinade. Cover with a lid and lower the heat to low. Cook for 2 minutes. Serve the cod over the steamed rice, with the vegetables and sauce on top.

61) GRILLED HALIBUT WITH AVOCADO SAUCE

Preparation Time: 10 minutes	Cooking Time: 10 minutes	Servings: 2

✓ Canola oil spray ✓ 2 (6-ounce / 170-g) halibut fillets ✓ 2 ripe avocados, peeled and pitted	✓ ½ cup sweet salsa verde ✓ ½ cup non-fat Greek yogurt ✓ 1 fresh jalapeño, seeded and diced
❖ Preheat grill pan. Lightly coat a grill pan with canola oil spray. Arrange the fillets on the pan. Mash the avocados and mix with the salsa, yogurt and jalapeño. Heat this mixture in a nonstick saucepan over low heat.	❖ Place the halibut fillets on the grill pan and cook for 5 minutes, then turn them over and cook for another 4 minutes. Serve the halibut with the warmed guacamole sauce on top.

62) SALMON AND AVOCADO COBB SALAD

Preparation Time: 20 minutes	Cooking Time: 12 minutes	Servings: 4

Salad: ✓ 1 pound (454 g) salmon fillets, skinless ✓ 1 tablespoon of olive oil ✓ ¼ teaspoon of kosher salt or sea salt ✓ ¼ teaspoon ground black pepper ✓ 6 cups chopped romaine lettuce ✓ 1 pint cherry tomatoes, halved ✓ 2 large hard-boiled eggs, peeled and cut into quarters ✓ 1 avocado, peeled and diced ✓ 2 shallots, thinly sliced	Seasoning: ✓ ⅓ cup of low-fat buttermilk ✓ 2 tablespoons of fat-free Greek yogurt ✓ 2 tablespoons of mayonnaise ✓ Zest and juice of ½ lemon ✓ 1 tablespoon chopped fresh herbs of your choice such as dill, parsley or chives ✓ 1 or 2 garlic cloves, peeled and chopped ✓ ½ teaspoon of hot sauce ✓ ½ teaspoon of ground black pepper ✓ ¼ teaspoon of kosher salt or sea salt
❖ Preheat the oven to 400°F (205°C). Place salmon fillets in a greased baking dish. Drizzle with olive oil and season with salt and black pepper. Roast for 8-12 minutes, until salmon flakes easily with a fork. Allow to cool slightly. ❖ Assemble four salads by evenly distributing romaine, cherry tomatoes, hard-boiled eggs, avocado and scallions on 4 large plates or in 4 large containers.	❖ Blend dressing ingredients until combined. ❖ Add dressing to salad and toss if serving immediately. Add the salmon fillets. If storing, store salmon fillets and salad in airtight containers for up to 3 days. Store dressing separately in small airtight containers.

63) MANDARIN ORANGE CHICKEN SALAD

Preparation Time: 20 minutes	**Cooking Time:** 12 minutes	**Servings: 4**

Ingredients:

Seasoning:
- ✓ ¼ cup sodium-free rice wine vinegar
- ✓ 1 tablespoon of sesame oil
- ✓ 1 tablespoon of honey
- ✓ 2 garlic cloves, peeled and chopped
- ✓ 1 inch fresh ginger, peeled and chopped
- ✓ ¼ teaspoon of kosher salt or sea salt

Salad:
- ✓ 1 tablespoon of canola oil
- ✓ 1 pound (454 g) boneless skinless chicken breasts

Ingredients:
- ✓ ¼ teaspoon of kosher salt or sea salt
- ✓ ¼ teaspoon ground black pepper
- ✓ 1 large Napa cabbage head, shredded
- ✓ 1 cup shredded red cabbage
- ✓ ½ cup shredded carrots
- ✓ ½ cup shelled edamame
- ✓ ½ cup sliced almonds
- ✓ 2 shallots, thinly sliced
- ✓ 1 (8-ounce / 227-g) can mandarin oranges, drained

Directions:

- ❖ Prepare the dressing
- ❖ Combine all dressing ingredients in a jar or bowl and shake or whisk to combine. Refrigerate until ready to use.

- ❖ Prepare the salad
- ❖ Heat the canola oil in a skillet over medium heat. Season the chicken breasts with the salt and black pepper and place them in the skillet. Cook 5 to 6 minutes per side, until the internal temperature reaches 165°F (74°C). Place on a cutting board for 5 to 10 minutes to cool and then thinly slice against the grain.
- ❖ In a large bowl, mix Napa cabbage, red cabbage, carrots and edamame with dressing. Divide among 4 bowls and top with the sliced chicken, almonds, scallions and mandarin oranges.

64) CHICKEN WALDORF SALAD

Preparation Time: 20 minutes	**Cooking Time:** 12 minutes	**Servings: 4**

Ingredients:
- ✓ ¼ cup of fat-free Greek yogurt
- ✓ 2 tablespoons of mayonnaise
- ✓ 2 tablespoons of Dijon mustard
- ✓ 1 tablespoon of honey
- ✓ ¼ teaspoon of kosher salt or sea salt

Ingredients:
- ✓ ¼ teaspoon ground black pepper
- ✓ 3 cups chopped cooked chicken breast
- ✓ 1 apple, diced
- ✓ 2 stalks of celery, diced
- ✓ 1 cup of green or red seedless grapes cut in half
- ✓ ¼ cup chopped walnuts

Directions:

- ❖ In a bowl, whisk together the yogurt, mayonnaise, Dijon mustard, honey, salt and black pepper. Add the cooked chicken, apple, celery, grapes and nuts.

- ❖ Store in airtight containers in the refrigerator for up to 3 days.

65) BOW TIE PASTA SALAD WITH CHICKEN AND STRAWBERRIES

Preparation Time: 10 minutes	**Cooking Time:** 20 minutes	**Servings: 6**

Ingredients:

Seasoning:
- ✓ 2 tablespoons of balsamic vinegar
- ✓ 1 tablespoon Dijon mustard
- ✓ 1 tablespoon of honey
- ✓ ¼ cup olive oil
- ✓ ¼ teaspoon of kosher salt or sea salt
- ✓ ¼ teaspoon ground black pepper

Ingredients:

Salad:
- ✓ 8 ounces (227 g) of whole grain bow tie pasta
- ✓ 1 tablespoon of canola oil
- ✓ ½ pound (227 g) boneless skinless chicken breasts
- ✓ ¼ teaspoon of kosher salt or sea salt
- ✓ ¼ teaspoon ground black pepper
- ✓ 1 quart of strawberries, hulled and sliced
- ✓ 1 cup fresh spinach
- ✓ ½ cup of mini fresh mozzarella balls
- ✓ ¼ cup sliced almonds

Directions:

- ❖ Prepare the dressing:
- ❖ In a large bowl, whisk together the dressing ingredients until combined. Taste and adjust seasoning if necessary.
- ❖ Prepare the salad:
- ❖ Bring a large pot of water to a boil. Cook pasta according to package directions.

- ❖ In the same pot, heat the canola oil over medium heat. Season the chicken breasts with the salt and black pepper. Saute the chicken for 6 to 7 minutes per side, until the internal temperature reaches 165°F (74°C). Place on a plate or cutting board to cool. Cut into bite-size pieces.
- ❖ Place the strawberries, spinach, mozzarella, cooled pasta and diced chicken in the bowl with the dressing and toss to combine. Refrigerate until chilled and sprinkle almonds on top before serving.

66) PANZANELLA SALAD WITH TOMATOES

Preparation Time: 15 minutes	**Cooking Time:** 8 minutes	**Servings: 4**

Ingredients:

- ✓ 1 small baguette, cubed (about 5 ounces / 142 g total)
- ✓ 3 tablespoons of olive oil, divided
- ✓ 2 or 3 large ripe tomatoes, cut into cubes
- ✓ 1 tablespoon of red wine vinegar

Ingredients:

- ✓ ¼ teaspoon of kosher salt or sea salt
- ✓ ¼ teaspoon ground black pepper
- ✓ ¼ cup fresh basil leaves, torn up

Directions:

- ❖ Preheat the oven to 400°F (205°C).
- ❖ Place the cubed baguette on a baking sheet and drizzle with half of the olive oil. Roast in the oven for 8 minutes, until crispy. Transfer the croutons to a bowl.

- ❖ In the bowl, add the tomatoes, red wine vinegar, salt, black pepper and remaining olive oil. Stir to combine and top with the fresh basil. Serve immediately.

67) CREAMY AVOCADO EGG SALAD

Preparation Time: 10 minutes	**Cooking Time**: 20 minutes	**Servings**: 4

Ingredients:

- ✓ 8 big eggs
- ✓ 2 avocados, peeled
- ✓ Zest and juice of ½ lemon

Ingredients:

- ✓ ¼ cup chopped Italian flat leaf parsley
- ✓ ¼ teaspoon of kosher salt or sea salt
- ✓ ¼ teaspoon ground black pepper

Directions:

- ❖ Place the eggs in a saucepan and cover with cold water. Bring to a boil, turn off the heat and place a fitted lid on top. Set a timer for 17-18 minutes. Drain hot water and pour cold water over eggs until cool. Remove the shells and discard. Cut eggs into smaller pieces.

- ❖ In a bowl, mash the avocado. Add the eggs to the bowl, lemon zest and juice, Italian parsley, salt and ground black pepper. Stir to combine and serve.

68) MIXED GREEN SALAD WITH PARMESAN

Preparation Time: 5 minutes	**Cooking Time**: 5 minutes	**Servings**: 4

Ingredients:

- ✓ ¼ cup of extra virgin olive oil
- ✓ 2 tablespoons fresh lemon juice
- ✓ ¼ teaspoon salt
- ✓ ¼ teaspoon freshly ground black pepper

Ingredients:

- ✓ 6 cups of loosely packed mixed vegetables
- ✓ ½ small red onion, thinly sliced
- ✓ 1 small cucumber, peeled and thinly sliced
- ✓ ¼ cup grated Parmesan cheese

Directions:

- ❖ In a small bowl, whisk together the oil, lemon juice, salt and pepper until well combined. Store the dressing in 4 dressing cups.

- ❖ In a large bowl, combine mixed greens, onion and cucumber. Divide salad among 4 medium containers. Top each with 1 tablespoon Parmesan cheese.
- ❖ To serve, toss the dressing and salad together.

69) COLESLAW WITH POPPY SEED DRESSING

Preparation Time: 10 minutes	**Cooking Time**: 5 minutes	**Servings**: 6

Ingredients:

- ✓ ½ cup low-fat Greek yogurt
- ✓ 2 tablespoons of apple cider vinegar
- ✓ ½ tablespoon of extra virgin olive oil
- ✓ 1 teaspoon poppy seeds
- ✓ 1 teaspoon sugar

Ingredients:

- ✓ 4 cups finely chopped and tightly packed cabbage
- ✓ 2 cups of broccoli salad
- ✓ 2 cups thinly sliced Brussels sprouts
- ✓ 6 tablespoons of dried blueberries
- ✓ 6 tablespoons of hulled pumpkin seeds

Directions:

- ❖ In a small bowl, whisk together the yogurt, vinegar, oil, poppy seeds and sugar until well combined. Store the dressing in 6 dressing cups.
- ❖ In a large bowl, mix together the kale, broccoli salad and Brussels sprouts.

- ❖ Divide vegetables among 6 large containers and top each salad with cranberries and pumpkin seeds.
- ❖ To serve, toss the vegetables with the poppy seed dressing to coat them.

70) WEDGE SALAD WITH BLUE CHEESE DRESSING

Preparation Time: 15 minutes	**Cooking Time**: 0 minutes	**Servings: 4**

Ingredients:

- ✓ 1 cup low-fat Greek yogurt
- ✓ Juice of ½ large lemon
- ✓ ¼ teaspoon freshly ground black pepper
- ✓ ¼ teaspoon salt

Ingredients:

- ✓ ⅓ cup of crumbled blue cheese
- ✓ 2 heads of romaine lettuce, with the stem cut, divided in half lengthwise
- ✓ 1 cup of grape tomatoes cut in half
- ✓ ½ cup of slivered almonds

Directions:

- ❖ In a small bowl, whisk together the yogurt, lemon juice, pepper, salt and blue cheese until well combined. Store the dressing in 4 dressing cups.

- ❖ Divide the lettuce halves and tomatoes among 4 large containers. Store the almonds separately.
- ❖ To serve, arrange a turbot head half on a plate and top with the grape tomatoes. Sprinkle with 2 tablespoons of almonds and drizzle with the salad dressing.

71) BLACK BEAN SALAD WITH AVOCADO SAUCE

Preparation Time: 15 minutes	**Cooking Time**: 0 minutes	**Servings: 4**

Ingredients:

- ✓ 1 head of romaine lettuce, chopped
- ✓ 1 (15-ounce / 425-g) can no salt added black beans, drained and rinsed
- ✓ 2 cups of fresh or frozen (thawed) corn kernels
- ✓ 2 cups of grape tomatoes cut in half
- ✓ 2 small avocados, halved and pitted
- ✓ 1 cup chopped fresh cilantro

Ingredients:

- ✓ 1 cup low-fat Greek yogurt
- ✓ 8 shallots, chopped
- ✓ 3 garlic cloves, quartered
- ✓ Zest and juice of 1 large lime
- ✓ ½ teaspoon of sugar

Directions:

- ❖ In a large bowl, combine the lettuce, beans, corn and tomatoes. Stir until well combined. Divide salad among 4 large containers.

- ❖ Place the avocado pulp in a blender or food processor. Add the cilantro, yogurt, scallions, garlic, lime zest and juice, and sugar. Blend until well combined. Divide the dressing among 4 dressing cups.
- ❖ To serve, toss the salad and dressing together.

72) THREE BEAN SALAD

Preparation Time: 5 minutes	**Cooking Time:** 5 minutes	**Servings: 6**

Ingredients:

- ✓ 1 (15-ounce / 425-g) can no salt added green beans, drained
- ✓ 1 (15-ounce / 425-g) can no salt added chickpeas, drained and rinsed
- ✓ 1 (15-ounce / 425-g) can of beans without added salt, drained and rinsed
- ✓ 1 medium red onion, cut into thin rings
- ✓ 2 stalks of celery, finely chopped
- ✓ ¾ cup finely chopped fresh parsley

Ingredients:

- ✓ ¼ cup of sugar
- ✓ ½ cup apple cider vinegar
- ✓ 3 tablespoons of extra virgin olive oil
- ✓ ½ teaspoon salt
- ✓ ½ teaspoon of freshly ground black pepper

Directions:

❖ In a large bowl, toss together the green beans, chickpeas, beans, onion, celery, and parsley.

❖ In a small bowl, whisk together the sugar, vinegar, oil, salt and pepper. Add this to the bean mixture and stir to coat completely. Divide among 6 containers.

73) ROASTED SALMON AND BUTTERNUT SQUASH SALAD

Preparation Time: 10 minutes	**Cooking Time:** 25 minutes	**Servings: 4**

Ingredients:

- ✓ 1 (16-ounce / 454-g) package of diced peeled pumpkin
- ✓ 4 tablespoons of extra virgin olive oil
- ✓ Salt and freshly ground black pepper, to taste
- ✓ 4 skinless salmon fillets (6 oz / 170 g each)
- ✓ 3 tablespoons fresh lemon juice

Ingredients:

- ✓ 2 garlic cloves, minced
- ✓ 1 tablespoon chopped fresh tarragon or 1 teaspoon dried
- ✓ 1 teaspoon Dijon mustard
- ✓ 8 cups baby spinach

Directions:

❖ Preheat the oven to 425ºF (220ºC). Line a baking sheet with aluminum foil.

❖ In a medium bowl, mix squash with 1 tablespoon olive oil, a pinch of salt and ¼ teaspoon pepper. Spread on the prepared baking sheet and roast, stirring once, for 15 minutes.

❖ Remove the baking sheet from the oven (leave the oven on) and move the squash to one side. Place salmon fillets on foil and sprinkle each with salt and pepper, if desired. Return to oven and bake until salmon flakes easily with a fork, 5 to 10 minutes, turning halfway through cooking.

❖ Meanwhile, in a small bowl, whisk together the lemon juice, remaining 3 tablespoons olive oil, garlic, tarragon, and Dijon mustard.

❖ In a large bowl, add the spinach and half of the vinaigrette and toss to combine. Portion the spinach onto 4 serving plates, add a quarter of the butternut squash and the salmon fillet. Drizzle with a little of the vinaigrette.

74) STRAWBERRY CHICKEN AND SPINACH SALAD

Preparation Time: 10 minutes	**Cooking Time**: 10 minutes	**Servings: 2**

Ingredients:

Chicken:
- ✓ 2 boneless, skinless chicken breasts (4 ounces / 113 g each)
- ✓ 1 garlic clove, crushed with the side of a knife
- ✓ Pinch of salt
- ✓ ½ tablespoon of extra virgin olive oil

Seasoning:
- ✓ 1 tablespoon of extra virgin olive oil
- ✓ 1 tablespoon of balsamic vinegar
- ✓ 1 teaspoon of honey
- ✓ 1 tablespoon finely chopped shallot

Ingredients:

- ✓ Freshly ground black pepper (optional)
- ✓ ¼ cup chopped fresh cilantro

Salad:
- ✓ Pinch of salt
- ✓ 1 cup instant peas, stalks trimmed and cut diagonally into ¼-inch pieces
- ✓ 6 cups bulk packed spinach
- ✓ 1 cup sliced strawberries
- ✓ ¼ cup sliced almonds

❖ Prepare the chicken: Season the chicken with the crushed garlic and salt.

❖ Heat a large skillet over medium heat and add the oil. When it shimmers, add the chicken and cook until it rises easily with a spatula, 4 to 5 minutes. Turn it over and continue cooking until a thermometer inserted in the center reads 165°F (74°C), another 4 to 5 minutes. Remove from pan and set aside until cool, then slice.

❖ Meanwhile, prepare the dressing: In a small bowl, whisk together the oil, vinegar, honey, 1 teaspoon water, shallot, black pepper, if desired, and cilantro.

❖ Prepare the salad: Bring a medium pot of water to a boil. Add the salt and instant peas and blanch until the peas are tender but still a little crisp, about 3 minutes. Drain and run under cold water and drain again. Pat dry to remove excess water.

❖ In a large bowl, mix together the peas, spinach, strawberries and almonds. Drizzle with the dressing and toss to combine.

❖ Divide salad between 2 serving plates. Slice the chicken and divide between the salads.

75) SHRIMP SALAD WITH GINGER VINAIGRETTE

Preparation Time: 10 minutes	**Cooking Time**: 3 minutes	**Servings: 2**

Ingredients:

Salad:
- ✓ 1 cup frozen green peas
- ✓ 8 ounces (227 g) cooked peeled and deveined shrimp, cut into ½ inch pieces
- ✓ 1 cup shredded carrots
- ✓ 1 medium red bell pepper, thinly sliced
- ✓ ¼ cup chopped cashews
- ✓ 2 tablespoons chopped shallot

Ingredients:

Ginger dressing:
- ✓ 2 tablespoons unseasoned rice vinegar
- ✓ 1 tablespoon of extra virgin olive oil
- ✓ ½ tablespoon of sesame oil
- ✓ 2 tablespoons fresh grated ginger
- ✓ 1 teaspoon of low-sodium soy sauce
- ✓ Pinch of red pepper flakes
- ✓ 6 cups mixed vegetables

❖ Prepare the salad: Bring a small pot of water to a boil. Add peas and blanch until tender but not mushy, about 3 minutes. Drain and rinse under cold water until cool. Drain on paper towels, then transfer to a medium bowl.

❖ In the bowl, add the shrimp, carrots, bell bell pepper, cashews, and scallions.

❖ Make the ginger dressing: In a small bowl, whisk together the vinegar, extra virgin olive oil, sesame oil, ginger, soy sauce and pepper flakes.

❖ Pour the dressing over the shrimp and vegetables and toss to coat.

❖ To serve, divide baby greens between 2 serving plates. Add half of the shrimp and vegetable mixture.

76) ENERGY QUINOA AND SPINACH SALAD

Preparation Time: 5 minutes	**Cooking Time**: 10 minutes	**Servings**: 2

Ingredients:

- ✓ ½ cup of quinoa, rinsed and drained
- ✓ 2 cups spinach, finely chopped
- ✓ 1 medium tomato, diced
- ✓ 1 cup sweet peas
- ✓ ½ cup diced cucumbers

Ingredients:

- ✓ ¼ cup sliced almonds
- ✓ ½ cup canned chickpeas, rinsed and drained
- ✓ 1½ tablespoon fresh lemon juice
- ✓ 1½ tablespoons of extra virgin olive oil
- ✓ ¼ teaspoon salt
- ✓ ¼ teaspoon freshly ground black pepper

Directions:

❖ In a medium saucepan, combine quinoa and 1 cup water and bring to a boil over medium-high heat. Reduce heat to a simmer, cover, and cook until quinoa has absorbed all the water, 10 to 15 minutes.

❖ Remove from heat, cover and let quinoa steam for 5 minutes. Remove the lid and stir with a fork.

❖ In a large bowl, combine the spinach, tomato, peas, cucumbers, almonds, chickpeas and cooled quinoa.

❖ In a small bowl, whisk together the lemon juice, olive oil, salt and pepper. Pour over the quinoa and vegetables and toss to coat.

❖ Portion into 2 serving bowls.

77) ZUCCHINI MOCK PASTA SALAD

Preparation Time: 15 minutes	**Cooking Time**: 15 minutes	**Servings**: 6

Ingredients:

Zucchini Tagliatelle:
- ✓ 2 large zucchini (about 22 ounces / 624 g)
- ✓ 1 tablespoon of extra virgin olive oil
- ✓ 2 garlic cloves, minced
- ✓ 1 large red bell pepper, thinly sliced and cut into 1-inch pieces

Seasoning:
- ✓ 1 tablespoon of extra virgin olive oil
- ✓ 1 large avocado
- ✓ ¼ cup of fat-free Greek yogurt (0%)

Ingredients:

- ✓ 2 teaspoons of fresh lemon juice
- ✓ 2 garlic cloves, minced
- ✓ 2 teaspoons of dried basil
- ✓ Salt and freshly ground black pepper, to taste (optional)

Salad:
- ✓ 2 cups frozen shelled edamame
- ✓ 1 cup of cherry tomatoes cut in half
- ✓ 1 (15-ounce / 425-g) can black beans, rinsed and drained
- ✓ 3 tablespoons of finely chopped chives

Directions:

❖ Prepare the zucchini noodles: Cut off the ends of the zucchini and spiralize them. Place zucchini noodles in a large bowl lined with paper towels to absorb excess moisture.

❖ In a large skillet, heat the olive oil over medium-high heat. Add the garlic, bell bell pepper, and spiralized zucchini. Cook until the vegetables are tender, being careful not to overcook, 6 to 8 minutes.

❖ Meanwhile, make the dressing: In a blender or food processor, combine the olive oil, avocado, Greek yogurt, ¼ cup water, lemon juice, garlic, basil, salt and pepper, if desired, and blend until smooth.

❖ Make the salad: Place edamame in a microwave-safe dish, add 1 to 2 tablespoons water, and cook over high heat until tender, 3 to 5 minutes. Drain and transfer to a large bowl.

❖ Add the zucchini noodle mixture, cherry tomatoes, black beans and chives to the bowl. Drizzle with the avocado dressing and toss to combine.

❖ Portion onto 6 plates.

78) HERB POLENTA

Preparation Time: 10 minutes	Cooking Time: 12 minutes	Servings: 6

✓ 1 cup polenta	✓ 2 teaspoons thyme, chopped
✓ 1/4 teaspoon nutmeg	✓ 2 teaspoons rosemary, chopped
✓ 3 tablespoons fresh parsley, chopped	✓ 2 teaspoons sage, chopped
✓ 1/4 cup milk	✓ 1 small onion, chopped
✓ 1/2 cup Parmesan cheese, grated	✓ 2 tablespoons olive oil Salt
✓ 4 cups vegetable broth	

Directions:

❖ Add the oil to the inner pot of the robot and set the pot to sauté mode. Add the onion and herbs and sauté for 4 minutes.

❖ Add the polenta, broth and salt and stir well.

❖ Close the pot with the lid and cook on high heat for 8 minutes. Once done, allow the pressure to release naturally.

❖ Remove the lid. Stir in the remaining ingredients and serve.

79) BUFFALO QUINOA BITES

Preparation Time:	Cooking Time: 15 minutes	Servings: 4

✓ 2 cups cooked quinoa	✓ 1 egg
✓ 1 cup shredded mozzarella cheese	✓ 1/4 cup chopped cilantro
✓ 1/2 cup buffalo sauce	✓ 1 small onion, diced
✓ 1/4 cup +1 tablespoon flour	

Directions:

❖ Preheat oven to 350oF. Mix all ingredients together in a large bowl. Press mixture into greased mini muffin pans.

❖ Bake for about 15 minutes or until bites are golden brown. Enjoy on their own or with blue cheese or ranch dressing.

80) RED WINE RISOTTO

Preparation Time:	Cooking Time: 25 minutes	Servings: 8

✓ Pepper to taste	✓ 1 ½ cups Italian "risotto" rice
✓ 1 cup finely shredded Parmigiano-Reggiano cheese, divided	✓ 2 cloves garlic, minced
✓ 2 tablespoons tomato paste	✓ 1 medium onion, freshly chopped
✓ 1 ¾ cups dry red wine	✓ 2 tablespoons extra-virgin olive oil
✓ ¼ teaspoon salt	✓ 4 ½ cups low-sodium beef broth

❖ Over medium-high heat, bring broth to a boil in a medium skillet. Lower the heat so that the broth is steaming but not boiling.

❖ Over medium low heat, place a Dutch oven and heat the oil. Sauté the onions for 5 minutes. Add the garlic and cook for 2 minutes. Add the rice, mix well and season with salt. In the rice, add a generous splash of wine and ½ cup of broth.

❖ Lower the heat to a simmer, cook until the liquid is completely absorbed, stirring the rice occasionally. Add another splash of wine and ½ cup of broth. Stirring occasionally. Add tomato paste and stir to mix well.

❖ Continue to cook and add wine and broth until the broth is used up. When finished cooking, turn off the heat and stir in pepper and ¾ cup cheese. To serve, sprinkle with remaining cheese and enjoy.

Chapter 4. THE

BEST RECIPES

81) SPRING PASTA

Preparation Time: 25 minutes	**Cooking Time**:	**Servings: 4**

✓ 2 cups cauliflower florets, cut into matchsticks ✓ 16 ounces tortiglioni ✓ ¼ cup olive oil ✓ ½ cup fresh green onions, chopped ✓ 1 red bell bell pepper, thinly sliced	✓ 4 cloves garlic, chopped ✓ 1 cup grape tomatoes, halved ✓ 2 tablespoons dried Italian dressing ✓ ½ lemon, squeezed ✓ ½ cup grated Pecorino Romano cheese
❖ In a pot of boiling water, cook tortiglioni for 8-10 minutes until al dente. Drain and set aside. Heat the olive oil in a skillet and sauté the onion, cauliflower and bell bell pepper for 7 minutes.	❖ Add the garlic and cook until fragrant, 30 seconds. Stir in tomatoes and Italian seasoning; cook until tomatoes are softened, 5 minutes. ❖ Add lemon juice and tortiglioni and adjust taste with salt and black pepper. Garnish with pecorino romano cheese.

82) DELICIOUS CHICKEN PASTA

Preparation Time: 10 minutes	**Cooking Time**: 17 minutes	**Servings: 4**

✓ 3 chicken breasts, skinless, boneless, cut into pieces ✓ 9 ounces whole-wheat pasta ✓ 1/2 cup olives, sliced ✓ 1/2 cup sun-dried tomatoes	✓ 1 tablespoon roasted red peppers, chopped ✓ 14 ounces tomatoes, diced ✓ 2 cups marinara sauce ✓ 1 cup chicken broth Pepper Salt
❖ with the lid and cook on high heat for 12 minutes. ❖ Once done, allow the pressure to release naturally. Remove the lid. Add the pasta and stir well. Seal the pot again and select manual and set the timer for 5 minutes.	❖ Once done, allow pressure to release naturally for 5 minutes then release the remaining using quick release. Remove the lid. Stir well and serve.

83) TASTY MAC & CHEESE

Preparation Time: 10 minutes	**Cooking Time**: 10 minutes	**Servings: 6**

✓ 16 ounces whole-wheat elbow pasta ✓ 4 cups water ✓ 1 cup canned tomatoes, diced ✓ 1 tablespoon garlic, minced ✓ 2 tablespoons olive oil ✓ 1/4 cup green onions, chopped ✓ 1/2 cup Parmesan cheese, grated ✓ 1/2 cup mozzarella cheese, grated	✓ 1 cup cheddar cheese, grated ✓ 1/4 cup passata ✓ 1 cup unsweetened almond milk ✓ 1 cup marinated artichokes, diced ✓ 1/2 cup sun-dried tomatoes, sliced ✓ 1/2 cup olives, sliced ✓ 1 teaspoon salt
Directions: ❖ Add the pasta, water, tomatoes, garlic, oil and salt to the Instant Pot and mix well. Close the pot with the lid and cook on high heat for 4 minutes. ❖ Once done, let the pressure release naturally for 5 minutes then release the rest using the quick release. Remove the lid. Set the pot to sauté mode.	❖ Add the green onion, parmesan, mozzarella, cheddar cheese, passata, almond milk, artichoke, sun-dried tomatoes and olive. Mix well. ❖ Stir well and cook until cheese is melted. Serve and enjoy.

84) RISOTTO WITH AROMATIC HERBS

Preparation Time: 10 minutes	**Cooking Time**: 15 minutes	**Servings: 4**

- ✓ 2 cups rice
- ✓ 2 tablespoons Parmesan cheese, grated
- ✓ 3.5 ounces heavy cream
- ✓ 1 tablespoon fresh oregano, chopped
- ✓ 1 tablespoon fresh basil, chopped
- ✓ 1/2 tablespoon sage, chopped
- ✓ 1 onion, chopped
- ✓ 2 tablespoons olive oil
- ✓ 1 tablespoon garlic, chopped
- ✓ 4 cups vegetable broth Pepper Salt

❖ Add the oil to the inner pot of the Instant Pot and set the pot to sauté mode. Add the garlic and onion and sauté for 2-3 minutes.

❖ Add the remaining ingredients except the parmesan cheese and heavy cream and mix well. Close the pot with the lid and cook on high heat for 12 minutes.

❖ Once done, allow the pressure to release naturally for 10 minutes then release the rest using the quick release. Remove the lid. Add the cream and cheese and serve.

85) DELICIOUS SPRING PASTA

Preparation Time: 10 minutes	**Cooking Time**: 4 minutes	**Servings: 4**

- ✓ 8 ounces whole wheat penne pasta
- ✓ 1 tablespoon fresh lemon juice
- ✓ 2 tablespoons fresh parsley, chopped
- ✓ 1/4 cup chopped almonds
- ✓ 1/4 cup Parmesan cheese, grated
- ✓ 14 ounces tomatoes, diced
- ✓ 1/2 cup prunes
- ✓ 1/2 cup zucchini, chopped
- ✓ 1/2 cup asparagus, cut into 1-inch pieces
- ✓ 1/2 cup carrots, chopped
- ✓ 1/2 cup broccoli, chopped
- ✓ 1 3/4 cups vegetable broth Pepper Salt

❖ Add the broth, pars, tomatoes, plums, zucchini, asparagus, carrots and broccoli to the robot and mix well.

❖ Close the pot with the lid and cook on high heat for 4 minutes.

❖ Once done, release the pressure using the quick release.

❖ Remove the lid. Add the remaining ingredients and mix well and serve.

86) ROASTED PEPPER PASTA

Preparation Time: 10 minutes	**Cooking Time**: 13 minutes	**Servings: 6**

Ingredients:

- ✓ 1 pound whole-wheat penne pasta
- ✓ 1 tablespoon Italian seasoning
- ✓ 4 cups vegetable broth
- ✓ 1 tablespoon garlic, minced

Ingredients:

- ✓ 1/2 onion, chopped
- ✓ 1 jar roasted red peppers
- ✓ 1 cup feta cheese, crumbled
- ✓ 1 tablespoon olive oil Pepper Salt

Directions:

❖ Add the roasted bell bell pepper to the blender and blend until smooth. Add the oil to the inner pot of the Instant Pot and set the pot to sauté mode.

❖ Add the garlic and onion and sauté for 2-3 minutes. Add the blended roasted bell bell pepper and sauté for 2 minutes.

❖ Add remaining ingredients except feta cheese and mix well. Close the pot with the lid and cook on high heat for 8 minutes. Once done, allow pressure to release naturally for 5 minutes then release the rest using the quick release.

❖ Remove the lid. Add the feta cheese and serve.

87) MACARONI AND CHEESE

Preparation Time: 10 minutes	**Cooking Time**: 4 minutes	**Servings**: 8

Ingredients:

- ✓ 1 pound whole wheat pasta
- ✓ 1/2 cup Parmesan cheese, grated
- ✓ 4 cups cheddar cheese, shredded
- ✓ 1 cup milk

Ingredients:

- ✓ 1/4 teaspoon garlic powder
- ✓ 1/2 teaspoon ground mustard
- ✓ 2 tablespoons olive oil
- ✓ 4 cups water Pepper Salt

❖ • Add the pasta, garlic powder, mustard, oil, water, pepper and salt to the robot. Close the pot with the lid and cook on high heat for 4 minutes

❖ • Once done, release the pressure using the quick release. Remove the lid. Add remaining ingredients and mix well and serve

88) PASTA WITH TUNA

Preparation Time: 10 minutes	**Cooking Time**: 8 minutes	**Servings**: 6

Ingredients:

- ✓ 10-ounce canned tuna, drained
- ✓ 15 ounces whole-wheat rotini pasta
- ✓ 4 ounces mozzarella, diced
- ✓ 1/2 cup Parmesan, grated
- ✓ 1 teaspoon dried basil
- ✓ 14-ounce canned tomatoes, diced
- ✓ 4 cups vegetable broth

Ingredients:

- ✓ 1 tablespoon garlic, minced
- ✓ 8 ounces mushrooms, sliced
- ✓ 2 zucchini, sliced
- ✓ 1 onion, chopped
- ✓ 2 tablespoons olive oil Pepper Salt

❖ Add the oil to the inner pot of the Instant Pot and set the pot to sauté mode. Add the mushrooms, zucchini and onion and sauté until the onion is softened.

❖ Add the garlic and sauté for one minute. Add the pasta, basil, tuna, tomatoes and broth and mix well. Close the pot with the lid and cook on high heat for 4 minutes.

❖ Once done, let the pressure release naturally for 5 minutes then release the rest using the quick release.

❖ Remove the lid. Add the remaining ingredients, stir well and serve.

89) PASTA WITH OLIVES VEGAN

Preparation Time: 10 minutes	**Cooking Time**: 5 minutes	**Servings**: 4

Ingredients:

- ✓ 4 cups whole wheat penne pasta
- ✓ 1/2 cup olives, sliced
- ✓ 1 tablespoon capers
- ✓ 1/4 teaspoon red pepper flakes

Ingredients:

- ✓ 3 cups water
- ✓ 4 cups pasta sauce, homemade
- ✓ 1 tablespoon garlic, minced Pepper Salt

Directions:

❖ Add all ingredients to the inner pot of the robot and mix well. Seal the pot with the lid and cook on high for 5 minutes.

❖ Once done, release the pressure using the quick release. Remove the lid. Stir and serve

90) ITALIAN MACARONI AND CHEESE

Preparation Time: 10 minutes	**Cooking Time**: 6 minutes	**Servings**: 4

Ingredients:

- ✓ 1 lb whole wheat pasta
- ✓ 2 tablespoons Italian seasoning
- ✓ 1 1/2 teaspoons garlic powder
- ✓ 1 1/2 teaspoons onion powder

Ingredients:

- ✓ 1 cup sour cream
- ✓ 4 cups water
- ✓ 4 oz Parmesan cheese, shredded
- ✓ 12 oz ricotta cheese Pepper Salt

Directions:

- ❖ Add all ingredients except ricotta to the inner pot of the robot and mix well. Seal the pot with the lid and cook on high for 6 minutes.

- ❖ Once done, allow the pressure to release naturally for 5 minutes then release the rest using the quick release.
- ❖ Remove the lid. Add the ricotta cheese and mix well and serve.

91) DELICIOUS GREEK CHICKEN PASTA

Preparation Time: 10 minutes	**Cooking Time**: 10 minutes	**Servings**: 6

Ingredients:

- ✓ 2 chicken breasts, skinless, boned and cut into pieces
- ✓ 1/2 cup olives, sliced
- ✓ 2 cups vegetable broth

Ingredients:

- ✓ 12 ounces Greek vinaigrette dressing
- ✓ 1 pound whole-wheat pasta Pepper Salt

Directions:

- ❖ Add all ingredients to the inner pot of the robot and mix well. Seal the pot with the lid and cook on high heat for 10 minutes.

- ❖ Once done, release the pressure using the quick release. Remove the lid. Stir well and serve.

92) PASTA WITH SPINACH PESTO

Preparation Time: 10 minutes	Cooking Time: 10 minutes	Servings: 4

Ingredients:

- ✓ 8 ounces whole wheat pasta
- ✓ 1/3 cup grated mozzarella cheese
- ✓ 1/2 cup pesto
- ✓ 5 ounces fresh spinach

Ingredients:

- ✓ 1 3/4 cups water
- ✓ 8 ounces chopped mushrooms
- ✓ 1 tablespoon olive oil Pepper Salt

Directions:

- ❖ Add the oil to the inner pot of the robot and set the pot to sauté mode. Add the mushrooms and sauté for 5 minutes.
- ❖ Add the water and pasta and stir well. Close the pot with the lid and cook on high heat for 5 minutes.

- ❖ • Once done, release the pressure using the quick release. Remove the lid. Stir in remaining ingredients and serve

93) PASTA WITH PESTO AND SHRIMPS

Preparation Time: 15 minutes	Cooking Time:	Servings: 4

Ingredients:

- ✓ ¼ cup pesto, divided
- ✓ ¼ cup Parmesan cheese flakes
- ✓ 1 ¼ pounds large shrimp, shelled and seeded

Ingredients:

- ✓ 1 cup grape tomatoes cut in half
- ✓ 4 ounces angel hair pasta, cooked, rinsed and drained

- ❖ Over medium-high heat, place a large nonstick skillet and grease with cooking spray. Add the tomatoes, pesto and shrimp. Cook for 15 minutes or until shrimp are opaque while covered.

- ❖ Add the cooked pasta and cook until heated through. Transfer to a serving dish and garnish with Parmesan cheese.

94) HAM AND FAGGIOLI

Preparation Time: 15 minutes	Cooking Time:	Servings: 4

Ingredients:

- ✓ 12 ounces pasta, cooked and drained Pepper and salt to taste
- ✓ 3 tablespoons fresh chopped chives
- ✓ 3 cups arugula or watercress leaves, loosely packed
- ✓ ½ cup chicken broth, hot
- ✓ 1 tablespoon herb garlic butter

Ingredients:

- ✓ ½ cup Tuscan pecorino cheese, shredded
- ✓ 4 ounces prosciutto, chopped
- ✓ 2 cups cherry tomatoes, halved
- ✓ 1 19-ounce can of white beans, rinsed and drained

- ❖ Heat the grassy garlic butter, cheese, ham, tomatoes and beans in a large saucepan over medium low heat for 2 minutes.
- ❖ Once the mixture is simmering, stir constantly to melt the cheese while gradually stirring in the broth.

- ❖ Once the cheese is completely melted and incorporated, add the chives, arugula, pepper and salt.
- ❖ Turn off the heat and add the cooked pasta. Serve and enjoy.

95) RAVIOLI WITH RICOTTA AND SPINACH

Preparation Time: 15 minutes	**Cooking Time:**	**Servings: 2**

Ingredients:

- ✓ 1 cup chicken broth
- ✓ 1 cup frozen spinach, thawed
- ✓ 1 batch pasta
- ✓ 3 tablespoons heavy cream

Ingredients:

- ✓ 1 cup cottage cheese
- ✓ 1 ¾ cups spinach
- ✓ 1 small onion, finely chopped
- ✓ 2 tablespoons butter

❖ Create the filling: In a skillet, sauté onion and butter for about five minutes. Add spinach leaves and continue to cook for another four minutes. Remove from heat, drain liquid and chop onion and leaves.

❖ Then combine with 2 tablespoons of cream and the cottage cheese making sure it is well combined. Add pepper and salt to taste. With your dough, divide it into four balls.

❖ Roll out one ball to ¼ inch rectangular thickness. Cut a 1 ½ inch by 3 inch rectangles. Place the filling in the center of the rectangles, about 1 tablespoon and brush the filling with cold water.

❖ Fold the rectangles in half, making sure no air is trapped inside and seal with a cookie cutter. Use all of the filling.

❖ Create the pasta sauce: Until smooth, whisk together the chicken stock and spinach. Pour into the heated skillet and cook for two minutes. Add 1 tablespoon of cream and season with pepper and salt. Continue cooking for one minute and turn off the heat.

❖ Cook the ravioli by immersing them in a pot of boiling water with salt. Cook until al dente and then drain. Then quickly transfer the cooked ravioli to the pan of pasta sauce, toss to combine and serve.

96) PASTA WITH SEAFOOD AND VEGETABLES

Preparation Time:	**Cooking Time:** 20 minutes	**Servings: 4**

Ingredients:

- ✓ ¼ tsp. pepper
- ✓ ¼ tsp. salt
- ✓ 1 lb. shelled raw shrimp
- ✓ 1 lemon, cut into wedges
- ✓ 1 tbsp. butter 1 tbsp. olive oil
- ✓ 2 5-ounce cans chopped clams, drained (reserve 2 tablespoons clam juice)

Ingredients:

- ✓ 2 tablespoons dry white wine
- ✓ 4 cloves garlic, minced
- ✓ 4 cups spiralized zucchini (use a vegetable spiralizer)
- ✓ 4 tablespoons Parmesan cheese Fresh chopped parsley for garnish

Directions:

❖ Prepare zucchini and spiralize with a vegetable spiralizer. Arrange 1 cup of zucchini noodles per bowl. Total of 4 bowls. Over medium heat, place a large nonstick saucepan and heat oil and butter. For 1 minute, sauté garlic.

❖ Add shrimp and cook for 3 minutes until opaque or cooked through. Add the white wine, reserved clam juice and clams.

❖ Bring to a boil and continue to simmer for 2 minutes or until half the liquid has evaporated.

❖ Stir constantly. Season with pepper and salt. And if necessary, add more to taste. Remove from heat and distribute seafood sauce evenly among 4 bowls. Add one tablespoon of Parmesan cheese per bowl, serve and enjoy

97) SIMPLE PENNE APPETIZER

Preparation Time:	Cooking Time: 15 minutes	Servings: 4

Ingredients:

- ✓ ¼ cup pine nuts, toasted
- ✓ ½ cup grated Parmigiano-Reggiano cheese, divided
- ✓ 8oz penne pasta, cooked and drained
- ✓ 1 6oz jar artichoke hearts drained, sliced, marinated and cut into quarters

Ingredients:

- ✓ 1 7oz jar sun-dried tomatoes drained and cut in half packed in oil
- ✓ 3oz chopped prosciutto
- ✓ 1/3 cup pesto ½ cup pitted and chopped Kalamata olives
- ✓ 1 medium red bell pepper

Directions:

- ❖ Slice the bell bell pepper, discard the membranes, seeds and stem. On a foil-lined baking sheet, place the bell pepper halves, press down by hand and bake for eight minutes.
- ❖ Remove from oven, place in a sealed bag for 5 minutes before peeling and chopping.

- ❖ Place chopped bell bell pepper in a bowl and toss with artichokes, tomatoes, ham, pesto and olives.
- ❖ Add ¼ cup cheese and the pasta. Transfer to a serving dish and top with ¼ cup cheese and pine nuts. Serve and enjoy!

98) TASTY LASAGNA ROLLS

Preparation Time: 20 minutes	Cooking Time:	Servings: 6

Ingredients:

- ✓ ¼ teaspoon crushed red pepper
- ✓ ¼ teaspoon salt
- ✓ ½ cup shredded mozzarella cheese
- ✓ ½ cup Parmesan cheese, shredded
- ✓ 1 14-ounce package tofu, cubed
- ✓ 1 25-ounce can low-sodium marinara sauce

Ingredients:

- ✓ 1 tablespoon extra-virgin olive oil
- ✓ 12 whole-grain lasagna noodles
- ✓ 2 tablespoons Kalamata olives, chopped
- ✓ 3 cloves garlic, chopped
- ✓ 3 cups spinach, chopped

Directions:

- ❖ Put enough water in a large pot and cook lasagna noodles according to package instructions. Drain, rinse and set aside until ready to use. In a large skillet, sauté the garlic over medium heat for 20 seconds. Add the tofu and spinach and cook until the spinach wilts.
- ❖ Transfer this mixture to a bowl and add the Parmesan olives, salt, red pepper and 2/3 cup marinara sauce. In a skillet, spread 1 cup of the marinara sauce on the bottom.

- ❖ To make the rolls, place the noodles on a surface and spread ¼ cup of the tofu filling. Roll up and place on the pan with the marinara sauce. Do this process until all the lasagna noodles are rolled. Place the skillet over high heat and bring to a boil.
- ❖ Reduce heat to medium and let cook for three more minutes. Sprinkle with mozzarella cheese and allow the cheese to melt for two minutes. Serve hot.

99) TASTY MUSHROOMS BOLOGNESE STYLE		
Preparation Time: 65 minutes	**Cooking Time**:	Servings: 6

Ingredients:

- ✓ ¼ cup chopped fresh parsley oz Parmigiano-Reggiano cheese, grated
- ✓ 1 tablespoon kosher salt
- ✓ 10 oz whole wheat spaghetti, cooked and drained
- ✓ ¼ cup milk
- ✓ 1 14-ounce can whole peeled tomatoes
- ✓ ½ cup white wine
- ✓ 2 tablespoons tomato paste
- ✓ 1 tablespoon minced garlic
- ✓ 8 cups finely chopped cremini mushrooms

Ingredients:

- ✓ ½ pound ground pork meat
- ✓ ½ teaspoon freshly ground black pepper, divided
- ✓ ¾ teaspoon kosher salt, divided
- ✓ 2 ½ cups chopped onion
- ✓ 1 tablespoon olive oil
- ✓ 1 cup boiling water
- ✓ ½ oz dried porcini mushrooms

Directions:

- ❖ Leave porcini in a bowl of boiling water for twenty minutes, drain (reserve liquid), rinse and chop. Set aside. Over medium-high heat, place a Dutch oven with olive oil and cook the pork, ¼ tsp pepper, ¼ tsp salt and onions for ten minutes. Stir constantly to break up the ground pork pieces.
- ❖ Stir in ¼ teaspoon pepper, ¼ teaspoon salt, garlic and cremini mushrooms. Continue cooking until the liquid has evaporated, about fifteen minutes. Stirring constantly, add porcini and sauté for one minute.

- ❖ Add the wine, porcini liquid, tomatoes and tomato paste. Allow to simmer for forty minutes. Stir occasionally.
- ❖ Pour in the milk and cook for another two minutes before removing from the heat. Stir in the pasta and transfer to a serving dish. Garnish with parsley and cheese before serving

100) VEGETARIAN PASTA WITH SHRIMP, BASIL AND LEMON		
Preparation Time:	**Cooking Time**: 5 minutes	Servings: 4

Ingredients:

- ✓ 2 cups spinach
- ✓ ½ teaspoon salt
- ✓ 2 tablespoons fresh lemon juice
- ✓ 2 tablespoons extra virgin olive oil
- ✓ 3 tablespoons drained capers

Ingredients:

- ✓ ¼ cup chopped fresh basil
- ✓ 1 pound large peeled and hulled shrimp
- ✓ 4 cups spiralized zucchini

Directions:

- ❖ Divide among 4 serving plates, top with ¼ cup spinach, serve and enjoy.

101)   ROASTED BEET, AVOCADO AND WATERCRESS SALAD

Preparation Time: 15 minutes	**Cooking Time:** 1 hour	**Servings: 4**

Ingredients:

- ✓ 1 bunch (about 1½ pounds / 680 g) of golden beets
- ✓ 1 tablespoon of extra virgin olive oil
- ✓ 1 tablespoon of white wine vinegar
- ✓ ½ teaspoon of kosher salt
- ✓ ¼ teaspoon freshly ground black pepper

Ingredients:

- ✓ 1 bunch (about 4 ounces / 113 g) of watercress
- ✓ 1 avocado, peeled, pitted and diced
- ✓ ¼ cup of crumbled feta cheese
- ✓ ¼ cup of toasted walnuts
- ✓ 1 tablespoon chopped fresh chives

Directions:

- ❖ Preheat the oven to 425°F (220°C). Wash and trim the beets (cut an inch above the root of the beet, leaving the long tail if desired), then wrap each beet individually in aluminum foil. Place beets on a baking sheet and roast until fully cooked, 45 to 60 minutes depending on the size of each beet. Begin checking at 45 minutes; if it pierces easily with a fork, the beets are cooked.

- ❖ Remove the beets from the oven and let them cool. Under cold running water, remove the skin. Cut beets into cubes or wedges.
- ❖ In a large bowl, whisk together the olive oil, vinegar, salt and black pepper. Add the watercress and beets and mix well. Add the avocado, feta, walnuts and chives and toss gently.

102)   QUINOA, ZUCCHINI AND RADISH SALAD

Preparation Time: 20 minutes	**Cooking Time:** 20 minutes	**Servings: 4**

Quinoa:
- ✓ 1½ cups of water
- ✓ 1 cup of quinoa
- ✓ ¼ teaspoon of kosher salt

Salad:
- ✓ 2 tablespoons of extra virgin olive oil
- ✓ 1 zucchini, cut into thin rounds
- ✓ 6 small radishes, sliced

- ✓ 1 shallot, julienned
- ✓ ¾ teaspoon of kosher salt
- ✓ ¼ teaspoon freshly ground black pepper
- ✓ 2 garlic cloves, sliced
- ✓ Zest of 1 lemon
- ✓ 2 tablespoons of lemon juice
- ✓ ¼ cup chopped fresh mint
- ✓ ¼ cup chopped fresh basil
- ✓ ¼ cup shelled and roasted pistachios

- ❖ Prepare the quinoa
- ❖ Bring the water, quinoa and salt to a boil in a medium saucepan. Reduce to a simmer, cover and cook for 10-12 minutes. Stir with a fork.
- ❖ Prepare the salad

- ❖ Heat the olive oil in a large skillet or frying pan over medium-high heat. Add the zucchini, radishes, shallots, salt and black pepper and saute for 7 to 8 minutes. Add the garlic and cook for another 30 seconds to 1 minute.
- ❖ In a large bowl, combine the lemon zest and lemon juice. Add the quinoa and mix well. Add the cooked zucchini mixture and mix well. Add the mint, basil and pistachios and toss gently.

103) ITALIAN WHITE BEAN SALAD		
Preparation Time: 15 minutes	**Cooking Time**: 0 minutes	**Servings**: 4
✓ 2 tablespoons of extra virgin olive oil ✓ 2 tablespoons of white wine vinegar ✓ ½ shallot, chopped ✓ ½ teaspoon of kosher salt ✓ ¼ teaspoon freshly ground black pepper	✓ 2 stalks of celery, diced ✓ ½ red bell pepper, diced ✓ ¼ cup fresh chopped parsley ✓ ¼ cup chopped fresh mint ✓ 3 cups cooked cannellini beans, or 2 cans (15-ounce / 425-g) cannellini beans with no added salt or low sodium, drained and rinsed	
❖ In a large bowl, whisk together the olive oil, vinegar, shallot, salt and black pepper.	❖ Add the beans, celery, red bell pepper, parsley and mint; mix well.	

104) CANTUCCI TOSCANI		
Prep Time: 1 hour 25 minutes	**Cooking Time**:	**Servings**: 20 cantucci
✓ Zest of 1 lemon ✓ 3/4 cup slivered almonds ✓ 2 cups flour ✓ 3/4 cup sugar ✓ 1 teaspoon baking powder	✓ ¼ teaspoon salt ✓ 3 eggs ✓ 1 teaspoon olive oil ✓ 2 tablespoons Amaretto liqueur	
❖ Preheat oven to 280°F. Combine the flour, baking powder, sugar, lemon zest, salt and almonds in a bowl and mix well. In another bowl, beat the eggs and amaretto liqueur.	❖ Pour into the flour mixture and stir to combine. Grease a baking sheet with olive oil and spread the dough. Bake for 40-45 minutes. Remove from oven, let cool for a few minutes and cut diagonally into slices about 1/2 inch thick. ❖ Place the pieces back on the sheet, cut sides up, and bake for another 20 minutes. Allow to cool before serving.	

105) MAPLE GRILLED PINEAPPLE		
Preparation Time: 10 minutes	**Cooking Time**:	**Servings**: 4
Ingredients: ✓ 1 tablespoon maple syrup ✓ 1 pineapple, peeled and cut into wedges	Ingredients: ✓ ½ teaspoon cinnamon powder	
Directions: ❖ Preheat a grill over high heat. Place fruit in a bowl and drizzle with maple syrup; sprinkle with ground cinnamon.	❖ Grill for about 7-8 minutes, turning occasionally until fruit cracks slightly. Serve.	

106) TRADITIONAL GREEK DUMPLINGS WITH HONEY AND PISTACHIOS

Preparation Time: 25 minutes	**Cooking Time**:	**Servings**: 4

Ingredients:

- ½ cup warm milk
- 2 cups flour
- 2 eggs, beaten
- 1 teaspoon sugar
- 1 ½ oz active dry yeast
- 1 cup warm water

Ingredients:

- ½ teaspoon vanilla extract
- 1 teaspoon cinnamon
- 1 orange, peeled
- 1 cup vegetable oil
- 4 tablespoons honey
- 2 tablespoons pistachios, chopped

Directions:

- ❖ In a bowl, sift the flour and combine with the cinnamon and orange zest. In another bowl, mix the sugar, yeast and ½ cup warm water. Let sit until the yeast dissolves.
- ❖ Stir in the milk, vanilla extract and flour mixture. Beat with an electric mixer for 1-2 minutes until smooth. Cover the bowl with plastic wrap and let rise in a warm place for at least 1 hour. Pour the vegetable oil into a deep skillet or wok to come halfway up the sides and heat the oil. Add more oil if needed.

- ❖ Using a teaspoon, form balls, one by one, and drop them into the hot oil one by one. Fry the balls on all sides, until golden brown. Remove them with a slotted spoon onto paper towels to absorb excess grease. Repeat the process until the dough is used up. Drizzle with honey and sprinkle with pistachios to serve.

107) SPICY STUFFED APPLES

Preparation Time: 55 minutes	**Cooking Time**:	**Servings**: 4

Ingredients:

- 2 tablespoons brown sugar
- 4 apples, core
- ¼ cup chopped pecans

Ingredients:

- 1 teaspoon cinnamon powder
- ¼ teaspoon nutmeg powder
- ¼ teaspoon ginger powder

- ❖ Preheat oven to 375 F. Arrange apples cut side up on a baking sheet. Combine the pecans, cinnamon, brown sugar and nutmeg in a bowl. Pour the mixture into the apples and bake for 35-40 minutes until golden brown. Serve immediately.

108) APPLE DATE BLEND

Preparation Time: 10 minutes	**Cooking Time**: 15 minutes	**Servings: 4**

Ingredients:

- ✓ 4 apples, cored and cut into pieces
- ✓ 1 teaspoon vanilla
- ✓ 1 teaspoon cinnamon

Ingredients:

- ✓ 1/2 cup pitted dates
- ✓ 1 1/2 cups apple juice

Directions:

- ❖ Add all ingredients to the inner pot of the robot and mix well. Seal the pot with the lid and cook on high heat for 15 minutes.

- ❖ Once done, allow the pressure to release naturally for 10 minutes then release the remaining using the quick release. Remove the lid. Stir and serve.

109) SPECIAL COCOA BROWNIE BOMBS

Preparation Time: 15 minutes	**Cooking Time**: 25 minutes	**Servings: 12**

Ingredients:

- ✓ 2 tablespoons grass-fed almond butter
- ✓ 1 whole egg
- ✓ 2 teaspoons vanilla extract
- ✓ ¼ teaspoon baking powder

Ingredients:

- ✓ 1/3 cup heavy cream
- ✓ 3/4 cup almond butter
- ✓ ¼ cup cocoa powder
- ✓ A pinch of sunflower seeds

Directions:

- ❖ Crack eggs and beat with a whisk until smooth. Add all the wet ingredients and mix well. Make the batter by mixing all the dry ingredients and sifting in the wet ingredients.

- ❖ Pour into a greased baking dish. Bake for 25 minutes at 350 degrees F or until a toothpick inserted in the center comes out clean. Let cool, cut into slices and serve.

110) MINI MINT HAPPINESS

Preparation Time: 45 minutes	**Cooking Time**: 2 hours	**Servings: 12**

Ingredients:

- ✓ 2 teaspoons vanilla extract
- ✓ 1 ½ cups coconut oil
- ✓ 1 ¼ cups almond butter with sunflower seeds
- ✓ ½ cup dried parsley

Ingredients:

- ✓ 1 teaspoon peppermint extract
- ✓ A pinch of sunflower seeds 1 cup dark chocolate chips
- ✓ Stevia to taste

Directions:

- ❖ Melt together the coconut oil and dark chocolate chips in a double boiler. Take a food processor, add in all the ingredients and pulse until smooth. Pour into round molds. Allow to freeze.

111) GENEROUS MAPLE AND PECAN BITES

Preparation Time: 10 minutes	**Cooking Time**: 25 minutes + freezing	**Servings: 12**

Ingredients:

- ✓ 1 cup almond flour
- ✓ ½ cup coconut oil
- ✓ ½ cup flaxseed meal
- ✓ ½ cup unsweetened chocolate chips

Ingredients:

- ✓ 2 cups pecans, chopped
- ✓ ½ cup unsweetened maple syrup
- ✓ 20-25 drops Stevia

❖ Take a baking sheet and sprinkle pecans on top. Bake at 350 degrees F until aromatic. This usually takes about 6 to 8 minutes. Meanwhile, sift together all the dry ingredients. Add the toasted pecans to the mix and mix well.

❖ Add the coconut oil and maple syrup. Mix to make a thick, sticky mixture. Take a loaf pan lined with parchment paper and pour the mixture into it. Bake for about 18 minutes. Cut into slices and serve.

112) FANTASTIC BROWNIE MUFFINS

Preparation Time: 10 minutes	**Cooking Time**: 35 minutes	**Servings: 5**

Ingredients:

- ✓ 1 cup golden flaxseed meal
- ✓ ¼ cup cocoa powder
- ✓ 1 tablespoon cinnamon
- ✓ ½ tablespoon baking powder
- ✓ ½ teaspoon sunflower seeds
- ✓ 1 large whole egg

Ingredients:

- ✓ 2 tablespoons coconut oil
- ✓ ¼ cup unsweetened caramel syrup
- ✓ ½ cup pumpkin puree
- ✓ 1 teaspoon vanilla extract
- ✓ 1 teaspoon apple cider vinegar
- ✓ ¼ cup almonds, shelled

❖ Preheat oven to 350 degrees F. Take a bowl and add all of the listed ingredients and mix well. Take the desired number of muffin pans and line them up with paper liners.

❖ Spoon the batter into the muffin pans, filling them up to about 1/4 of the liner. Sprinkle a few almonds on top. Place them in your oven and bake for 15 minutes. Serve warm.

113) SIMPLE GINGERBREAD MUFFINS

Preparation Time: 5 minutes	**Cooking Time**: 30 minutes	**Servings: 12**

Ingredients:

- ✓ 1 tablespoon ground flaxseed
- ✓ 6 tablespoons coconut almond milk
- ✓ 1 tablespoon apple cider vinegar
- ✓ ½ cup peanut almond butter

Ingredients:

- ✓ 2 tablespoons gingerbread spice blend
- ✓ 1 teaspoon baking powder
- ✓ 1 teaspoon vanilla extract
- ✓ 2 tablespoons Swerve

❖ Preheat the oven to 350 degrees F. Take a bowl and add the flax seeds, sweetener, sunflower seeds, vanilla, spices and your non-dairy almond milk. Set it aside for a bit.

❖ Add the peanut almond butter, baking powder and continue to mix until well combined. Stir in the peanut almond butter and baking powder. Mix well.

❖ Spoon the mixture into muffin liners. Bake for 30 minutes. Let them cool and enjoy!

114) NUTMEG NOUGATS

Preparation Time: 10 minutes	Cooking Time: 5 minutes + 30 minutes freezing time	Servings: 12

Ingredients:

- ✓ 1 cup coconut, shredded
- ✓ 1 cup low-fat cream

Ingredients:

- ✓ 1 cup cashew almond butter
- ✓ ½ teaspoon nutmeg powder

Directions:

- ❖ Melt the cashew and almond butter in a double boiler. Add nutmeg and cream cheese. Remove from heat. Allow to cool a bit. Keep in the refrigerator for at least 30 minutes.

- ❖ Remove from refrigerator and make small balls. Coat with shredded coconut. Let cool for 2 hours and then serve.

115) RASPBERRY SUPREME CHOCOLATE BOMBS

Preparation Time: 10 minutes	Cooking Time: /[MOU2] Freezing Time: 1 hour	Servings: 6

Ingredients:

- ✓ ½ cocoa almond butter
- ✓ ½ coconut manna
- ✓ 4 tablespoons coconut milk powder

Ingredients:

- ✓ 3 tablespoons granulated stevia
- ✓ ¼ cup dried and crushed raspberries, frozen

Directions:

- ❖ Prepare double boiler over medium heat and melt cocoa almond butter and coconut manna. Stir in the vanilla extract. Take another pot and add the coconut powder and sugar substitute.

- ❖ Stir the coconut mixture into the cocoa butter, 1 tablespoon at a time, making sure to keep stirring after each addition. Add the crushed dried raspberries. Mix well and distribute into muffin pans. Chill for 60 minutes and enjoy!

116) CASHEW AND ALMOND BUTTER

Preparation Time: 5 minutes	Cooking Time:	Servings: 1

Ingredients:

- ✓ 1 cup almonds, blanched
- ✓ 1/3 cup cashews
- ✓ 2 tablespoons coconut oil

Ingredients:

- ✓ Sunflower seeds as needed
- ✓ ½ teaspoon cinnamon

Directions:

- ❖ Preheat oven to 350 degrees F. Bake almonds and cashews for 12 minutes. Allow them to cool.

- ❖ Transfer to food processor and add remaining ingredients. Add oil and continue blending until smooth. Serve and enjoy!

117) ELEGANT CRANBERRY MUFFINS

Preparation Time: 10 minutes	**Cooking Time:** 20 minutes	**Servings: 24 muffins**

Ingredients:

- ✓ 2 cups almond flour
- ✓ 2 teaspoons baking soda
- ✓ ¼ cup avocado oil
- ✓ 1 whole egg
- ✓ ¾ cup almond milk

Ingredients:

- ✓ ½ cup erythritol
- ✓ ½ cup applesauce
- ✓ Zest of 1 orange
- ✓ 2 teaspoons cinnamon powder
- ✓ 2 cups fresh blueberries

Directions:

❖ Preheat oven to 350 degrees F. Line muffin pan with paper cups and set aside. Add the flour, baking soda and set aside. Take another bowl and whisk the remaining ingredients and add the flour, mix well.

❖ Pour the batter into the prepared muffin pan and bake for 20 minutes. Once done, let cool for 10 minutes. Serve and enjoy!

118) FASHIONABLE CHOCOLATE PARFAIT

Preparation Time: 2 hours	**Cooking Time:**	**Servings: 4**

Ingredients:

- ✓ 2 tablespoons cocoa powder
- ✓ 1 cup almond milk
- ✓ 1 tablespoon chia seeds

Ingredients:

- ✓ Pinch sunflower seeds
- ✓ ½ teaspoon vanilla extract

Directions:

❖ Take a bowl and add the cocoa powder, almond milk, chia seeds, vanilla extract and mix. Transfer to a dessert glass and refrigerate for 2 hours. Serve and enjoy!

119) MESMERIZING AVOCADO AND CHOCOLATE PUDDING

Preparation Time: 30 minutes	**Cooking Time:**	**Servings: 2**

Ingredients:

- ✓ 1 avocado, chopped
- ✓ 1 tablespoon natural sweetener such as stevia
- ✓ 2 ounces cream cheese, room temperature

Ingredients:

- ✓ ¼ teaspoon vanilla extract
- ✓ 4 tablespoons cocoa powder, unsweetened

Directions:

❖ Blend listed ingredients in blender until smooth. Divide the mixture between dessert bowls, chill for 30 minutes. Serve and enjoy!

120)   HEALTHY BERRY TART

Preparation Time: 10 minutes	**Cooking Time:** 2 hours 30 minutes	**Servings: 8**

Ingredients:

- ✓ 1 ¼ cups almond flour
- ✓ 1 cup coconut sugar
- ✓ 1 teaspoon baking powder
- ✓ ½ teaspoon cinnamon powder
- ✓ 1 whole egg

Ingredients:

- ✓ ¼ cup low-fat milk
- ✓ 2 tablespoons olive oil
- ✓ 2 cups raspberries
- ✓ 2 cups blueberries

Directions:

- ❖ Take a bowl and add the almond flour, coconut sugar, baking powder and cinnamon. Mix well. Take another bowl and add the egg, milk, oil,

---

121)   SPICED POPCORN

Preparation Time: 2 minutes	**Cooking Time:**	**Servings: 4**

Ingredients:

- ✓ ½ teaspoon of chili powder
- ✓ ⅛ teaspoon of garlic powder without salt
- ✓ ⅛ teaspoon of paprika

Ingredients:

- ✓ ⅛ teaspoon of cayenne
- ✓ 8 cups of air popped popcorn

Directions:

- ❖ In a small bowl, combine the chili powder, garlic powder, paprika and cayenne.

- ❖ Place popcorn in a large bowl and toss with the spice mixture. Serve immediately or store in an airtight container for up to 2 days.

---

122)   BAKED TORTILLA CHIPS WITH LIME

Preparation Time: 5 minutes	**Cooking Time:** 25 minutes	**Servings: 6**

Ingredients:

- ✓ 4 teaspoons of lime juice
- ✓ 2 teaspoons of canola oil
- ✓ ½ teaspoon of ground cumin

Ingredients:

- ✓ 12 corn tortillas (6 inches)
- ✓ Kitchen spray

Directions:

- ❖ Preheat oven to 400°F (205°C). Spray two large baking sheets with cooking spray.
- ❖ In a small bowl, mix together the lime juice, canola oil and cumin. Brush each tortilla on both sides with the mixture and cut into 6 wedges

- ❖ Arrange the tortilla pieces in a single layer on the prepared baking sheets. Bake in the preheated oven, rotating the pans every 10 minutes, until the chips are golden brown and potato chip, about 25 minutes.

Bibliography

FROM THE SAME AUTHOR

DASH DIET FOR HER *Cookbook* - More than 120 recipes for Women to reduce Cholesterol and Triglycerides! Start a Healthier lifestyle and Stop Hypertension with a Dietary Approach!

DASH DIET FOR BEGINNERS *Cookbook* - The Simplest and Quickest 120+ Dietary approach recipes to Stop Hypertension! Increase your heart health and reduce cholesterol and triglycerides with one of the healthiest diets overall!

DASH DIET FOR ONE *Cookbook* - More than Healthy 110 recipes to stop hypertension and reduce cholesterol! Stay Healthy and increase your body Wellness with the Best Dishes for One!

DASH DIET FOR HEALTHY KIDS' HEART *Cookbook* - More than 120 recipes for the health of your kids! Prevent Hypertension and Hearth Disease in your Children with one of the Best Diet Overall!

DASH DIET FOR TWO *Cookbook* - The Best 220+ Healthy Recipes to cook with your partner! Taste yourself and your love with many heart-health recipes for couple!

DASH DIET FOR HEALTHY COUPLE *Cookbook* - More than 220 Recipes for Two to reduce triglycerides and cholesterol! Delight Yourself and Your Partner with the Healthiest Dietary Approach Recipes!

DASH DIET FOR MUM & KIDS *Cookbook* - The Best 220+ Healthy and Quick Recipes to cook with your Kids! Delight yourself and your children and increase your heart health with the best Dietary Approach Recipes!

DASH DIET FOR START YOUR NEW HEALTHY LIFESTYLE *Cookbook* - More than 220 really health Recipes to Start by NOW the Dietary Approach. Increase your heart-health and reduce cholesterol and triglycerides with this Simple and Fantastic Diet!

DASH DIET FOR CHOLESTEROL CONTROL *Cookbook* - The Best 220+ Recipes to Reduce Bad Fat, Triglycerides, and Hypertension and Start to Have a New and Healthier Lifestyle!

Conclusion

Thanks for reading "Dash Diet for Beginners Cookbook"!
Follow the right habits it is essential to have a healthy
Lifestyle, and the Dash diet is the best solution!

I hope you liked this Cookbook!
I wish you to achieve all your goals!

Michelle Sandler

CPSIA information can be obtained
at www.ICGtesting.com
Printed in the USA
BVHW010941040621
608627BV00024B/499